MOUNTAIN TRACE

Book II

MOUNTAIN TRACE

Book II

Edited by
Kenneth Gilbert

With a Foreword by
David A. Bice

Illustrated by
Steve Harrison

Jalamap Publications, Inc.
Charleston, West Virginia

Jalamap Publications, Inc., 833 Scenic Drive, Charleston, WV 25311
©1983 by Jalamap Publications, Inc.
All rights reserved
Printed in the United States of America
Library of Congress Number 80-80065
ISBN 0-934750-19-X

To:
Those students who have spent hundreds of extra
hours to make our project a success and to my mother.

Contents

Part One: Lumbering
- Henderson Sharp ... 2
- Emment Taylor ... 15
- Bill Harper ... 31
- Markwood Gum ... 44
- Cass, A Lumber Town ... 54

Part Two: Arts & Crafts
- The Art of Teneriffe Embroidery ... 59
- Rug Braiding ... 65
- Playing the Dulcimer ... 67
- Making the Dulcimer ... 71
- Bill Reed, Wood Carver ... 81
- Appalachian Recipes ... 88
- Candle-making ... 92
- Harold Reed, Printer ... 95
- Making An Applehead Doll ... 108
- George Pinkham, Wood Craftsman ... 116
- Making A Corncob Doll ... 126

Part Three: Folklore
- Home Remedies ... 134
- Old Wives Tales ... 140
- Superstitions ... 143

Part Four: Recollections
- Spring Harvest Dinner, with Edelene Wood ... 146
- Wild Food Recipes ... 148
- The Greatest Show on Earth ... 152
- Louise Butcher, Teacher at Spruce ... 164
- Making Swiss Cheese ... 169
- Streetcars of Parkersburg and Marietta ... 175
- Colonel Joseph Barker ... 192
- Terrapin Park ... 210
- Mr. Helmick ... 214

Borland Springs Hotel	225
Sonnencroft	229
Mrs. Thelma Shaw	240
Appendix	245
Index of Students	245
Index of Contacts	246
Glossary	249

Foreword

One of the most important aspects of any society is the recording of its past. Knowledge of where one is going is built on the firm foundations of where one has been. MOUNTAIN TRACE BOOK II provides us with a part of that foundation. This is not a history book in the classical sense but a book of historical glimpses.

Mr. Ken Gilbert, his assistants, and the students in the MOUNTAIN TRACE classes at Parkersburg High School, Parkersburg, West Virginia have given us a collection of stories which will enrich not only our lives, but for many of us, our memories. They have provided us the opportunity to look back to an earlier time and relive the times of our grandparents.

It is important to realize that the stories have been gathered and written by high school students. These students have honored their heritage by pursuing and capturing the past. Through this book, a learning situation in a high school has become a TRACE or trail for us to follow.

As you read these pages savor the odors, sights and sounds of our past.

— the sweet smell of freshly cut timber
— trolley wheels clickity-clacking
— the purgent puffs of smoke from a steam engine
— the buzz of a saw shaping cherry wood
— the beauty of structure in an old mansion
— the tinkling of a dulcimer
— the smell of a country kitchen

You will find many more delights for your senses throughout the book.

This work provides us the opportunity to engage in the highest level of reading, that of enjoyment. The charge to all readers is just that, enjoy! Do not analyze, philosophize or categorize. Simply, enjoy!

David A. Bice

Preface

Our research for MOUNTAIN TRACE Book II has taken us to many new areas, or traces, throughout West Virginia. Since the timber industry played such a vital role in the development of the state, we have spent time in Pocahontas County interviewing many former timbermen. We felt fortunate to be able to meet with Henderson Sharp and discuss the logging industry before the days of the railroad. Mr. Sharp was on the last log drive down the Greenbrier River in 1908. One can't help but have a feeling of nostalgia as he remembers the hardships of such a drive. He relates stories such as the one about a fellow timberman who lost his leg as he fell between the logs. We can laugh with him as he recalls Adam Jones who pulled into the river while trying to hook the key log to pull the dam so that the drive could begin.

Emment Taylor reminisced about the winters in the lumber camps. One could return the next spring and see the butts of the trees six feet above the ground. The timber had been cut during the winter when the snow was deep. He recollects the bedbugs, the life at the lumber camp, and the ill-forebidden gambling that went on under the shanties at night.

A teacher remembers her feelings as she ventured by train to the top of Cheat Mountain to meet her first class at Spruce, once the highest city in the United States. She knew that she couldn't return home until the end of the week when she had to catch another log train down the mountain.

The fascination of our quest continued as we traveled to Webster County and were the guests of the Ballie sisters. While visiting on this remote farm, we learned of the family's decision to settle in the mountains as the result of a promise from a land grant agent that the countryside would be congruous to that of their native Switzerland. After a milking session and a tour of the farm, we learned the secret to making Swiss cheese according to a recipe that has been handed down for generations.

Other chapters include memories of the last streetcars, the demise of the tent circus, and the now extinct sulfur health spas. Along with these are fascinating articles filled with practical information pertaining to buggy wheel construction, candlemaking, woodcarving, teneriffe embroidery, and applehead or corncob doll creation.

As we sought out and experienced the past through the lives of our contacts, our concern has been to communicate this legacy to our readers.

Over the years many people have contributed to the success and survival of MOUNTAIN TRACE. Although we could never begin to recognize everyone who has assisted us, we do feel that it is necessary to mention a few of our benefactors.

First of all, we must acknowledge the parents of our students. They have permitted their sons and daughters to accompany us on field trips throughout West Virginia.

The teachers and administrators at Parkersburg High School have allowed us occasionally to disrupt the regular school schedule. To them, we owe our thanks. We also must mention the students and teachers who have developed and assisted with our project. Many students graciously gave more of their time and effort than we expected. We wish also to thank the three teachers, Susan Beckett, Scott Yoak, and Joan Myers, who have performed such general duties as maintaining the classroom and proofreading.

A special word of appreciation is necessary for our friends in Pocahontas County. All of our interviews concerning the timber industry were conducted among these gracious people. Ted and Linda Stuart helped to arrange both our interviews and our housing. The following people were kind enough to allow us to visit in their homes: Mr. and Mrs. Liptak, Mrs. Gum, Mr. and Mrs. Mullenix, and Mr. and Mrs. Monk. In addition, we wish to express our sincere gratitude to all of our contacts with whom we have experienced our heritage.

We also wish to extend our thanks to Susie Monk, Charles Leavitt, Nobel Schofield, Fred Mayer, and the Pocahontas Historical Society. Many of the priceless photographs reproduced in this volume were loaned to us by them.

Our sincere appreciation also goes to the Parkersburg Community Foundation for its support through monetary grants.

Finally, we wish to thank our readers who have supported MOUNTAIN TRACE since its inception.

KEN GILBERT

INTRODUCTION

In the introduction to MOUNTAIN TRACE Book I, we discussed our feelings toward the MOUNTAIN TRACE experience and our goals. We now remember our efforts during the past two years.

Our research has taken us to new areas, or traces, throughout West Virginia. Since the timber industry played such a vital role in the development of the state, we have spent much time in Pocahontas County interviewing many of the former timbermen. We felt fortunate to be able to meet with Henderson Sharp and discuss the logging industry before the days of the railroad. Mr. Sharp was on the last log drive down the Greenbrier River in 1908. One can't help but have a feeling of nostalgia as he remembers the hardships of such a drive. He relates stories such as the one about a fellow timberman who lost his leg as he fell between the logs. We can laugh with him as he recalls Adam Jones who was pulled into the river while trying to hook the key log to pull the dam so that the drive could begin.

Emment Taylor reminisced about the winters in the lumber camps. One could return the next spring and see the butts of the trees six foot above the ground. The timber had been cut during the winter when the snow was so deep. He recollects the bedbugs, the life at the lumber camp, and even the ill-forbidden gambling that went on under the shanties at night.

A teacher remembers her feelings as she ventured by train to the top of Cheat Mountain to meet her first class at Spruce (once the highest city in the United States). She knew that she couldn't return home until the end of the week when she had to catch another log train down the mountain.

The fascination of our quest continued as we traveled to Webster County and were the guests of the Ballie sisters. While visiting on this remote farm, we learned of the family's decision to settle in the mountains as the result of a promise from a land grant agent that the countryside would be congruous to that of their native Switzerland. After a milking session and a tour of the farm, we learned the secret to making Swiss cheese according to a recipe that has been handed down for generations.

Other chapters include memories of the last streetcars, the demise of the tent circus, and the now extinct sulfur health spas. Along with these are fascinating articles filled with practical information pertaining to buggy wheel construction, candlemaking, woodcarving, teneriffe embroidery, and applehead or corncob doll creation.

As we sought out and experienced the past through the lives of our contacts, our concern has been the communicate this legacy to our readers.

Although the purpose of the MOUNTAIN TRACE experience has been the recording of our oral heritage, we have been involved in many activities. Our staff has been in constant demand to speak at universities, colleges, elementary schools, junior highs, and high schools in west Virginia, Ohio, and Kentucky.

Speaking engagements have also taken us to civic and professional organizations throughout the state. Because of the MOUNTAIN TRACE project, Parkersburg High School was chosen by President Ford as one of the fourteen pilot schools in the United States to conduct a Youth/Elderly conference on such topics as housing, recreation, medical needs, life on a fixed income, and the acceptance of death. Senior citizens were invited to attend the conference and hear various guest lecturers. The culmination of the conference was an evaluation which was presented to Congress by president Ford as part of a study on the aged in America.

Ourstaff also was chosen tosubmit a chapter to the book, **I Wish I Could Give My Son a Wild Raccoon**, edited by Eliot Wigginton of FOXFIRE. This book was a bicentennial project for the Reading is Fundamental program at the Smithsonian Institution. We were also chosen as an official bicentennial project for thestate of West Virginia.

The sale of our magazines and books has extended to over sixty cities in West Virginia, thirty-two states, and eight foreign countries. MOUNTAIN TRACE has attained success on the local, regional, state, and national level. Success, for whatever value it holds, could not have been achieved without the consideration and laborious work of many.

Ourcontacts have been very patient with us and have allowed us to return many times for extra information. Our students have generously donated many hours to keep the program going. The administration of Parkersburg High School has constantly made loans to our program. Many times, the administration has given us moral support, even though we haven't always believed in ourselves. Readers have made contributions above the regular subscription prices simply because they believed in our efforts.

Susan Beckett, ScottYoak, and Joan Myers have assisted with the program in proofreading and other laborious work since the inception of the class in 1974.

To the many people who have given so much to carve and produce the beautiful state that we now enjoy, we hope topay homage by preserving a bit of our heritage through the printed word and the oral tradition. To them, their prayers, their determination, and their faith and courage, we offer our humble thanks.

Henderson Sharp

by Joan Carte and Donna Mollahan

Henderson Sharp of Frost, West Virginia, recalls life in the lumber camps at the turn of the century. He reflects on the river drives and admits that he knows no one else living who rode the river on the log drives. the last river drive went down the Greenbrier River in 1908. Our meeting with this 96 year old gentleman was delightful and rewarding. We hope that you will enjoy reminiscing with Henderson.

"I worked all up through this country in the timber industry, years ago. I drove logs down the Greenbrier River, down Knaps Creek and down Douthard's Creek and all around. I worked on Cheat Mountain for years. I worked for contractors, mainly. I worked for Mower Lumber Company at Cass. I worked for Shaffer at Cass He was the old original lumberman of Cass. He started at Cass about 1888, I expect — getting stuff out to build the town and the mills.

"My first job in the woods was cutting roads out for the teams. It was called swampin', and that was in 1908. From that, I went to cuttin' the trees. From that, I went to skiddin'. I drove teams all over this country. I drove team from over Pendleton County to Beard on the Greenbrier River at different times. Along about 1916-17, we were logging right here (Frost) in the county for the Warn Lumber Company. I moved here in 1900. I was born across the hill about a mile and a half from here. My father sold out over there and came here. I've been here ever since.

Henderson Sharp

"I was about sixteen when I started in the timber industry. I made a hand, made a hand right out with the men. We started peelin' hemlock over there in the Big Run. An old man Stauntan served an injunction on us to cut the peelin' down, around the last of July. But old man Huntly, he was the superintendent too, he was one of these bull-headed fellows, and you couldn't out do him. He went ahead and hired every man he could hire and got every short handled ax he could get, and we peeled that four million with axes — finished it out with axes, finished up late in January. Of course, they had been skiddin'. The teams had been skiddin' right after us all the time. We got it all to the landing down there, four million feet, right at the last of March, and there was a big snow on.

"There was an awful snow that winter. It was good skiddin' and slick. We'd turn out on Sunday night at midnight and go until Wednesday at noon. We'd just stop to eat and go back to work. We'd go in Wednesday at noon and sleep and go back out at 6:00 a.m. Thursday to work again. We did that until that four million feet was put into the creek at the landing. When we finished, the old boss man asked for volunteers to go up to Little Shumate, they called it, and peel enough to make two million feet in the pile there on the creek. Of course, we all volunteered and took the lanterns, teams, cutting crews and all, and went up to Shumate and cut those big hemlocks that stood up in there. We cut her that night and peeled her and brought her into the creek. We got that into the creek, and there was no sign of any rain. It was still snowing. The boss said, 'Now boys, go to the camp and eat, and you are on your own until it comes a thaw to raise the creek. When the creek raises so we can pull the landing and start 'em down the creek, all of you come back.'

"I was home just about two weeks until it began to rain. The snow melted and the creek began to raise. It was all over these bottoms, and we went to work on the drive. The foreman of the job knowed where the key log was in that pile of logs to pull to let the water through. We put this old man, Adam Jones, from Pennsylvania, down in there on that log, and the team swum in there with the spreaders on and the grabs were on the spreaders. Ben Campbell from up here at Dunmore was driving the team. He was riding that old team in there to pull that log. He touched one of the horses in the ribs with one of his heels just about the time Adam hooked the grab, and it pulled him off in the water over his head. Old Adam raised up and said, 'Jesus, Ben, what did you do that for?' Those horses would swim in there and pull that key log out.

Horses pulling logs — Picture loaned by Susan Monk

"I think we had seven teams on that drive. When a log would roll in (on the bank) where you couldn't roll it back by hand, then you (also) needed a team to pull them (back) in the water. I've seen (those horses) swim until the water was rolling over their backs. It seemed like they couldn't go, but still they was going. You had to have a good size team to do that. At that time there was good teams in this country. They used Percerons mostly, a few Clydesdales and a few Belgians. They were short-legged and heavy bodied; But the Percherons were usually long-legged and stood high in the air, heads up, and they was the best swimmers.

"We landed that (log drive) way down the river when the water fell. We had to lay off for a few days. It came another rain. We had splash dams across the creeks, and they would catch the water and hold it back. They'd hold the water up for days; then they'd open the gates, and that would turn a lot more water in. When you reached the river (and got the logs out of the creeks), there usually was no trouble. I never was on the river when they used the ark. They had arks earlier, and the men slept in each end, and they cooked in the center of them and everything. They also had an ark for the horses to go in. They'd anchor them to a substantial tree (along the bank) that wouldn't fall in that wasn't washed out in under it, so they would be safe.

"They drove the Greenbrier River from the head of the river up at Willowburn and Mill Dam. They drove it for years. Smith and Whiting, they was the big lumber company before my time.

"There was always a lot of us on the back of the log drive rolling in—keeping the logs rolled in. We followed it right in to Marlinton.

"Never, nobody got killed on the log drives he was on, and very few got crippled. You had to have cork shoes to ride the logs. I always wore the AA Cutters (brand name). A pair of them would last you three years. They wouldn't leak. You might get in over the top of them and get your feet wet, but they wouldn't leak. The spikes in the bottom would last you about a year.

"They used everybody they could get on a drive. They fired a lot

Picture of early arks — loaned by Pocahontas Historical Society.

Early loggers — Picture loaned by Susan Monk.

of them too. I've seen 'em call them over and say, 'You're no good,' and give them their money right there.

"I made a dollar seventy-five a day, daylight until dark. There wasn't no hours to it, just daylight until dark. On the log drives the only tool you used was a cant hook. And you just watched not to get drowned. If you lost the cant hook, it was five dollars. The company furnished the first one; but if you lost it in the river, it cost you five dollars.

"On one log drive, I fell off in the river out of sight, but I held on to my cant hook. Lots of times the logs would jam up, just heaps of them, piled up high. Then you'd have to send maybe eight or ten of these catty men in to loosen them up. That would happen often here on the creek. The banks wasn't too high; and if they started jamming, they'd pile way back up the valley. So, they'd send men in that was handy with a cant hook and that could ride a log to unjam them. It is pretty hard to ride in swift water. If you don't get the right kind of log, it will go under with you. You need a log with the big end ahead and as big a log as you can get. In rough water, they are hard to handle. They always kept (john) boats along if someone fell in the river. He stayed pretty close with you. A lot of places in the river, you would have cliffs and rocks that the men couldn't get around, and they used these boats to get the men around to the other side. Every now and then, you would see five or six men going down the river on one log with their cant hooks pushing like oars. As long as the logs were going all right, you could just stand there and ride.

"If they jammed up and you could get one picked out of there for the water to run through, the water would take them out. These old fellows that drove on the river knew what logs to loosen. Experience taught you which one to take out.

"Pine, hemlocks, spruce—your softwoods are the only ones that would float. Your hardwoods, white oaks and red oaks, would not float.

"The river had to be full and out of its banks to make a good drive. When the water was decreasing was your best driving, when the water was falling. The logs wasn't floating to shore then. They was all going down the middle of the stream. You could tell when it was starting to fall. All of your logs would start to the center. When it was raising, they would float out. There was a crew to roll in and a crew to ride.

"The older drivers would ride up front to keep things from jamming. When the timbering started, it started in Pennsylvania and those old timers followed it right on down through here.

"I never went clear into Ronceverte with any drive. The length of the drive depended on the weather and the amount of water. It might be the middle of June before they got all of the logs down there to Ronceverte. They could just go as far as the raise (waters) would carry them. Then you would just camp there (or go home if you felt it would be a long enough period of time) and wait for the next one. Ordinarily back then, we had deep snows and a lot of run off (in the spring). I've drove teams when the snow was so deep it ran through the horses' collars.

"The last log drive was in 1908. That was the last drive down Knaps Creek or down the Greenbrier River. After that, they used the railroads for the logs. I was on the last drive down the Greenbrier River. There was a big rock down there in the river. It stuck up in the air high. Henry Lynch was on the boat and he said, 'Boys, if I can get you around that rock, I'll go around her; and if I can't, I'll swim.' He went around it, and he brought us ashore, and we come out down below Beard. That was the last drive. A man by the name of Sam Sheets was on that drive and got his leg cut off when he fell down through the logs. He was always able to get around after that.

"To start the drive, they rolled the logs across the creek in tiers. They would have about twenty tiers. To build the tiers they would build slides (for logs to come off the mountain on) out of timber up the sides of the mountain. They were of hewed logs like a trough up the mountains.

"Then they would have water boys with barrels of water. They would have a certain beat (area of the slide to cover) to put the water on when it was freezing. Sometimes, there would be three beats (sometimes more). There was twenty-one teams on one job I was on, seven teams to the beat when we were sliding. We slid there for days and days, and nights and nights.

"We used trail chains, fifty or sixty feet long, on the log slides. The trail would be sometimes fifty or sixty logs. You had to use a pretty good log for the shove log because you might have a lot of little ones in there that wouldn't shove well. But, if you had a good log in the back with your trail chain, you could shove them. It was heavy, so it would push them.

"They used a jigger horse back in the woods to roll the logs into the

Early loggers — Picture loaned by Susan Monk.

landing. He would get a trail in there for the next team to take to the slide.

"Then when the logs went down the mountain, the landing men had to catch them on the fly. Then they would take the cant hooks and roll them out of the slide.

"The horses that we used in the camps belonged to the local people, and they hired them to the timber people—two dollars and a half each day, and their board. This included the harness.

"There was an old Frenchman that lived down the creek here that had seven or eight teams. They was poor, my dear sir; they was poor. He brought them up to the camp. Even though they were poor, they would pull every pound they could. They was there all winter, and they got in pretty good shape by spring. They worked from daylight to dark, too. I've seen horses fall right off their feet when they would get to the barn at night; they would be so tired and dead for sleep. After awhile, they'd wake up and go to the trough and eat their oats.

"In the winter we would have to put corks and toes on our horses' shoes. The blacksmith did that. The toe would be about four inches long; and back on the heel, you would have a cork turned down, and it would be sharp. On one foot it would be sharp one way, and on the other one it would be sharp the other way. I've seen horses cork (cut) themselves awful bad with those shoes. We never had much trouble with them though. We'd just run some tar in the cut and tie them up for a few days."

CAMP JOBS

"From here, for about ten miles down, was just white pine country —big white pine. They just took the butt logs off of the trees when they cut them. They just burned the rest. They burned up millions of feet to get rid of it. Millions and millions of white pine were burned. Those trees were about six foot on the stump. There was two crews that cut 120,000 feet in one day. Each crew had two saws. They'd take one out in the morning; and about ten o'clock, they'd get another one that was sharp. At noon, they'd take another one; and at three o'clock, they'd take another one. And one day the scales said they cut 120,000 feet.

"There was a right smart of an art to sawing. You didn't want to ride the saw, and you didn't want to push it too heavy to the other fellow. I went over to Edenwood, this side of Elkins, and went to cutting for a fellow over there. He gave me a North Carolinian for a buddy. He was big and long-legged and had long arms, and I wasn't very big. We went out, and it was big timber — the biggest I ever seen grow out of the ground. He said, 'Son, you are light. You just hold that handle and hold her steady, and I'll do the rest of her.' And he would. He'd just shove her from end to end and pull her from end to end. We cut there for days.

"You'd have a peeler after you, spuddin.' About every four feet, the ringer would put a ring around 'em. Then the spudder would come along and peel it. They never saved the bark then, just left it lay.

"They had a scaler. He would come along after you and measure the logs. We would cut 10,000-12,000 feet a day. With eight or ten crews cuttin', he had a job to keep it all measured up.

"They had a sawyer to sharpen the saws. If a saw was cuttin' good, I would keep it all day. I have carried a few of them in before noon if they wasn't cuttin' though. And I have broke a few that wouldn't cut. I would tell the sawyer, 'You can go up and get the pieces if you want

Early loggers — Picture loaned by Susan Monk.

them." I always used a Simmon saw when I would get it. Sagger ax was my choice for an ax.

"They had a camp doctor that lived at Raymond. Old Doctor Miller would come as he was needed. He would sometimes stop by about twice a week if he wasn't needed at the office.

"They never heard of the flu then. I never heard of a case of the flu, and very few people was sick. I remember when they took the white pine out. I was about five years old, I reckon. My mother and me was a goin' to the log camp one Sunday for dinner. We got the old horse out and rode down there. She knew several of the old hicks down there; they lived right around here. Craig Ashword that lived up here at Greenbank, he was down there, and he was pretty sick. The doctor was there, I forget which one, probably old Dr. Patterson from Huntersville. He nearly died, and they had to take him home. They didn't have no hospitals then."

LUMBER CAMPS

"We'd walk at night three or four miles by moonlight to get back to camp and walk back in the morning before daylight to where we had left the tools. Them was good old days. It was hard work, but we had fun.

"The bell would ring about six o'clock for supper in the evening— FIVE O'CLOCK IN THE MORNING. They used a piece of railroad steel hung up in a tree, and just pound it with a hammer. I worked at one camp, and that's the way they turned you out, by the steel in the morning, back in at noon, back in the evening. You could hear the thing four or five miles.

"They fed you the best grub. They had everything you wanted: beef twice a day; pork, usually for breakfast; always, biscuits for breakfast, light bread or rolls for dinner and supper.

"The best cook I ever eat after was up at the head of the river— fellow by the name of Paul Nelson. He'd have turkey, chicken, fish, cakes and everything that you can name.

"It depended on how bad they needed logs what holidays you got off—usually, no holidays. They all took Sunday off except for one place I worked on Green Mountain; the contractor there had a big job, and he worked every Sunday. He did turn in at noon on Wednesday and let the men and horses rest.

"It was steep down over that mountain, and you just pull them logs over so far and skip the grabs out of 'em and turn 'em loose over the hill. By spring, we had an awful pile of logs down there.

"You take old camp 7, 9, 11 and 12. Each of these camps run about 125 men. They would all sleep upstairs over the lobby in one big room. The room would be lined with beds. Some of them three deep. They just had cheap mattresses made of cotton on them. They had plenty of bed clothes. And if you was halfway decent, you could keep it clean. I've seen some of them so lousy though, you couldn't sleep for the lice. I've throwed a lot of shirts out the window, covered up with lice.

"When the old man Shaffer was in business, he numbered every camp. He didn't put names to them. When they cut out an area, they just built a new camp at the next place. Sometimes, they'd tear down the old ones if they hadn't been there too long, and take them and rebuild them. They would always send a new load of lumber up to build with though.

"They kept the train tracks laid ahead of where they were working, so they would be ready to move. They kept a bunch to work on the tracks all of the time. It was always swampy in that spruce country. You'd think you were on solid ground, and the next minute you'd be in mud up to your neck. You'd go through the turf. They had to chunk and haul rock to build railroad tracks. They'd also take small chunks of spruce and put under there. They would just build bridges over those areas. Italians built most all of the train tracks."

SNOWS

"In the winter of 1907, there was no work nowhere. Four of us went up to the lumber camps for a job. The snow was over our heads, and the floor of the lobby was just full of men looking for work, and they couldn't get work. The boss would come out and say, 'I'm sorry fellows, but I don't have a thing for any of you.' They'd light off for another camp. It would be the same thing. The lobbies were just full of men sleeping on the floor. I was lucky; I never had to sleep on the floor one night.

"You could go back up there the next year, and the stumps were higher than my head where they had cut the trees that winter. The snow was that deep. They were cutting there for the ground that winter before."

AGE LIMIT

"You could work as long as you wanted to, as long as you were able to carry an ax or a cant hook. I never did know of anybody being laid off on account of their age. The last few years, now, they wouldn't hire you if you was over fifty. In the old camps, it didn't matter.

"As the business moved out, the old wood hicks moved out too. When they finished up, they went from here to yonder."

Workers and horses at lumber camp — Picture loaned by Susan Monk.

Emment Taylor
by Billy Crites and Lisa Carpenter

Emment Taylor spent an evening with us recalling the lumber industry. There were no cars to drive to work, and he had a six mile walk to the top of the mountain every day.

"I've cut about all over this country; that is Virginia, West Virginia, Cheat Mountain, and everywhere. I started out as a ball hooter. That was where it was too steep for a team to get up when they cut them down and had them into logs. They would wait for a snow to come or the ground froze, and then they would send a couple of men with a cant hook and they'd sight the logs down the mountain. Maybe they (the logs) would be in (hit) fifteen trees before you got them to the bottom. But that is the way we put them down. They did that over here at Cass. When it was rocky, if the logs were laying around the hill sideways, you'd use the cant hook and turn it around and get it sighted right. When it ran against trees or hit something and turned sideways, then you had to knock it loose. We generally start about eight or ten logs at a time over the mountain. Then we'd go back and work the others down.

"Then I went to cutting trees. I worked for Glen Golford. He run the camp. Me and Merle Knottingham went to cutting together first. Then he went to driving team. Then me and my brother, Boice, cut. We would average around 8,000 feet a day with crosscuts. I doubt if this hollow would hold all that we cut if they was piled up. If you couldn't cut that much, you didn't stay very long. And you also put them in

Emment Taylor

shape for the team to get them. We made $1.25 per thousand. After you paid your board, that left you about seven dollars per day. We thought that was good money because the farmers couldn't pay over a dollar a day. That was all they was able to pay. It was a hard job at that time. You could take your clothes to the creek and wring them out at the end of the day, winter or summer. You had to keep at it, to make any money. Back in them days, they didn't cut any stuff under 15-16 inches. They only cut the old original timber. Lots of trees, you could get over a 1,000 feet. We cut one log once that you could stand by it and couldn't see over it. We took a six foot saw, and it didn't reach it. After we got in, we had to take one of the handles off and each one of us would take time-about sawing with one hand. They said that was the biggest tree that went into the mill. It was oak. It was so big they couldn't load it with the loader. They had to pick up one end and lay it on the car and then get the other end. There was one other one that was twenty-seven feet around. Now these are big trees for this country. They first decided it would cost too much to get it to the mill. The mill couldn't cut it, and they didn't cut it. Then the stavemill come in, and they cut it. They took dynamite, bored holes into it, and then dynamited it and busted it apart. They made staves out of it for barrels and stuff. It was twenty-seven feet. It was an oak and just as sound as a dollar. I measured it myself.

"When hemlock time come, the later part of May or June, the sap would come up in the hemlock, and they had a fitter that rung the hemlock trees—rung them clear around. Then they'd take a spud and go right around it. Then you'd have a whole piece of bark there. Then you'd pile it up in bark piles. They took sleds and horses and loaded the sleds with the bark and hauled it off to the railroads and sold it to the tanneries. They made an extract to tan hides.

"You had to wear cork shoes. With the corks you could just jump those logs like a squirrel. Those corks would hold you right where you hit. They had a cork set that they drove into your shoe soles. They had thick soles on the shoes then. Then they screwed the corks in. They would start on the ball of your foot and go clear around the outside. Then they would take another row in the inside of that and keep that up until they was in the middle of the shoe—just like sewing. Then they did the same thing to your heel. Now if you would step on a piece of bark, and it stuck to them corks, and you didn't know it, and you hit a log; then down you'd go. Your feet was gone out from under you. But, most of the time after you was used to 'em, you could tell when anything was stuck to the bottom of your foot. If you worked in the mud, it would stick to them. If you would step on somebody with them things, you could ruin them. They was tempered and hard and just as sharp as a needle. They was about ¾ of an inch out of your shoe. It was hard to break one. You could wear them all winter and summer, and you hardly ever lost one. They would cut right into ice. I haven't seen a pair for fifty years. They called them AA Cutters (brand name). If a young fellow had a pair of AA Cutters, he thought he was in style. They were similar to a hunting boot. The heel was about two/two and a half inches high, and the top was about twelve inches high. Then they come around with Bergermans. They had a sloping heel. Them is the only two shoes that I wore when I worked in the woods.

"These old women around the community would knit socks out of pure wool and spin it. Then they'd knit socks and sell them to you for about a dollar a pair. When you put a pair of them on and them boots, it could get to ten or fifteen below zero and you would never know it.

"I've worked in rain, sleet, snow — you never turned in for nothing then. My fingers has got so cold before. When you were cutting, you had your ax, your saw, your wedges, your sledge hammer, cant hook, and measuring pole. When you got all of them on your back, you had to use your hands and all of them tools cold. If you had to go a distance to the next tree, your fingers would just go to stinging. Well, I've jerked the oil bottle out of my pocket. We had to carry an oil bottle in our pocket. It held about a half of a pint of coal oil. Whenever we made a cut, we kept a peg in the end of the oil bottle with two little notches, so when you would sling it, it would go clear across your saw. It made the saw run easier. It helped to get the gum off of the saw. It didn't pull as hard as when you tried to saw without it. I've took that, and splashed it up against a tree, and strike one of those old-timey matches, stick my fingers in the flame for two or three seconds, warm them right up, and go right on to the next tree.

"We did our own notching and bumping. I did the notching, and my brother did the bumping. Of course, if it was a big knot, we would take the crosscut saw and saw it off. But, he would use the ax for everything else. He would bump them, cut the limbs off, so the team would get them and take them in. They had roads up and down the hill for the team.

"They had mostly all spruce over on Cheat Mountain. I drove team, drove grabs, and cut a little there. I've been all over all of these hardwood camps through the country here in West Virginia and Virginia."

LUMBER CAMPS

"The lobby hog would get the teamster up about an hour or an hour and a half before they would ring the bell to get the other fellows up. He would come in and tap you on the shoulder to get up. The teamster would curry and brush the horses of a morning and feed and harness them before breakfast. You fed the horses morning, noon, and evening. If a man went with a team having dirt or filth on them, he didn't stay long.

"They kept pretty strict order in the camps back then, but they still had a lot of fighting and so on. But, you went by the rules. You couldn't go to the table and cuss and raise the dickens around. You just ask for what you wanted and people would pass it. There was an old fellow at one camp. He got into an awful argument one time, and the boss came in the next meal, and he told everybody to sit down. Everybody had a certain place. They had a table thirty or forty feet long. They'd set coffeepots every so often — just kept them in reach of each other. They kept that up all the way down the table. When some-

Early loggers — Picture loaned by Susan Monk.

one would pick up the coffeepot, everybody would take their old tin cups, and one fellow could stick his cup under and then the next one until they was all full. When they would get the amount in the cup that they wanted, they would say 'good.' That meant to stop. This old man I was telling about got his cup under there, and he said, 'good.' He just kept pouring, and he said, 'Damn, I said good.' He said, 'If it's good, I'll give you a damn plenty of it.' That old man got so mad he got up from the table and left.

"They had as good of food in the camps that you ever sat down to. They didn't have all of these new kinds of food that they've got now— just country food, cereals of all kinds, potatoes, beef, and hog meat.

"We was setting at the table another time and this old Clyde Carpenter, he's dead now, and they got into an argument. They told him there was no talking at the table after that. Just ask for what you wanted, and that was it. Old Clyde wanted some corn flakes, and you could hear a pin drop in there, and he looked up at me and said, 'Emment, would you pass me them damn owl feathers over here?' He called corn flakes 'owl feathers.' If them old people liked you, they'd do anything in the world for you.

"The working men ate first. The cook and cookee waited on the men as they ate. Some of the bosses would eat off in a little house they had separate, but most of the bosses ate with the men. There was very few people that thought they was better than the working men. They treated you good, but you had to work."

CAMP BUILDINGS

"They generally built these camps about a hundred feet long. It would be two stories. You slept upstairs. They generally had two rows of beds up the center of the room. Someone's feet would be at your head. They'd leave an aisle about two feet wide to walk to the beds. I expect they'd be seventy or eighty men in that one room. When the lights went out, if anybody said anything, he'd get a cork shoe. They'd let her drive right at you. You couldn't keep them fellows awake. There was a lobby. A pair of stairs came down into the lobby. They had a lobby hog, and all he did was care for the fires. He kept a fire all night. He'd get you up in the morning. He just worked at night. He'd sweep the floors. The lobby would be about twenty feet square and have benches clear around it to set on. Everybody wasn't in there at one time. Some of the men would go up, lay around on their beds and talk.

"Then the cooks generally had a shack beyond the camp. The lobby hog kept the fire going in the cook room too. So, when the cooks came in, it was warm. It was usually attached to the lobby."

BEDBUGS

"Bedbugs! Back in them old camps bedbugs were thick. There was one (camp) over here on Back Creek. Now, this is the truth; I'd never seen the like of bedbugs. When you turned the lights off, them suckers would drop off the walls and hit you in the face. We reach up and get one and smack it — and stink! They are the stinkingest things in the world. People would carry them home from the camps. You couldn't get rid of them at all. They'd get all over the house.

"We had straw ticks on the beds. I've taken mine off the bed at night and went out and laid under the sugar trees to keep those bedbugs off of me, in the warm summer nights."

TIME SPENT AT CAMPS

"We'd stay on the mountain a couple of months before we'd come off. We'd think we had a devil of a stake. We'd have maybe fifty or sixty dollars to draw. Then you'd blow that and go back a couple of months longer and come out again. Some of them old fellers would stay up there a year at a time.

"We worked six days a week, ten hours a day. There wasn't no such thing as three or four hours a day. You started before daylight. I've stayed right over here, me and my brother, and we'd walk to the top of the Allegheny Mountain. I'd say it is close to six miles. I've walked to the top of a morning and get there at daylight to work, and the snow would be knee deep; I'd work all morning, then sit down to dinner. When we was close that away, we boarded at home at took our dinner. You'd pick that dinner up and the biscuits would be frozen as hard as a rock. We'd have to build a fire to thaw them out so we could eat them. We'd work ten hours, and then we'd walk back home at night. We'd walk her in the morning and evening. When we'd get there, it would be light enough to see to use your saw and ax. We'd stay right there until dark. It was all uphill going and all downhill coming home."

WEATHER

"The weather got so cold once, and they had four or five cats there at the camp. The creek came right up by the camp. I went out there one night, and a cat had stepped in the water and then stepped on a rock, and its foot just froze to the rock. I had to take cat, rock and all in to the stove. Now that is the truth. It froze him right there. He was just sitting there meowing."

GAMBLING

"There was an old fellow; he always called me, 'Boy.' He said, 'Boy, you want to get in the poker game tonight?' I said, 'I never did play poker.' He said, 'That is a good way to learn.' I said, 'I ain't got no money to play poker.' He said, 'I am going to give you ten dollars to start you off with.' That was a lot of money back then. He handed it to me. Well, I thought I'd get in that. I got in the penny ante game first. You could only bet a nickel. I got in it first. I got four or five dollars, and I thought I could play poker.

"Generally, the camps were built up off the ground three or four feet high. They was usually along streams. Then if the water got up, it would go under them instead of coming in. We'd go under them to play poker. You couldn't play in the lobby. They didn't allow that. You had to hide. I went down under there. I just got set down. I decided I would get some real money. And I did! They got mine in just about a minute. The old man asked me the next morning, 'Did you win anything?' I said, 'Hell, no, I didn't get set down until I had to get back up and leave.' They'd have four or five games going at once down there."

STEALING

"Hardly anybody ever stole anything. There was just nails around the wall, and you'd hang your clothes and things there. It generally hung right there. One time I had a shirt, similar to the Ritchie shirts now, and a pair of gloves stolen. That's the only time I ever had anything bothered. The lobby hog was there all of the time, and he sort of watched things."

PAY

"Sometimes they would pay you by the thousand. Then you had a scaler to measure the timber as you cut it. When we cut by the thousand, we got a dollar or a dollar and a quarter to cut hardwood. Then when you peeled, you got about seventy-five cents more on the thousand for spudding it off. If you come to what they called a red one, the bark was red, and they was hard to peel. We generally just skipped them. When the boss came around and wanted to know what was the matter with that one, I'd say, 'It's a red one.' He'd say, 'Let me have the spud, and I'll see if it's red.' We got the same scale for it if it was a red one. There was a lot of 'em that you couldn't gouge it off from. The sap wouldn't come up on them. But, we called a lot of them that we could've peeled too."

GETTING A JOB

"If you'd go to one camp, it might be filled up. Then you'd go to another one. It might be ten or fifteen miles. You walked it, walked the railroad ties. I've walked many and many a mile getting a job, but if you wanted a job you could generally wind up getting one. They tell you when you got there, they was sorry they didn't need no more men; or if they needed a couple of men, they'd tell you. They generally had your name down; they'd call your name, and you'd step out. They'd take you down to the office and sign you up. Then you'd go doing whatever they told you to do.

"Some of those old timber men would still be working when they was seventy/seventy-five years old. After they got old, they didn't do much sawin' and stuff, but they worked on the railroads with a mattock, swampin' for the teams. It was still a hard job, but they'd work. They'd put poles on the skidding roads. Then the logs would run easier on them, when they got on these poles. When they come to a turn, they'd put a log there so when your horses was coming, the logs wouldn't run into the bank. Them poles would keep shooting the logs out from the banks, and they wouldn't pull so hard. They knew how to make roads then. These old people would work at jobs like that till they was way up in years."

WOOD HICKS

"They was a lot of those old men that was never married that worked in the timber. They'd run from a woman. That was the kind that would stay in the camps and not come off. They'd stay until they died or got so durned old they couldn't go nowhere, and they'd go home and die. They'd never talk about a woman, never mention a woman. I think if you mentioned one to them, it would make them mad. I knowed a lot of them. They didn't care whether they came off the mountain or not. They usually had a lot of money 'cause they would never spend any.

"The only money they'd spend is sometimes they'd send an order down to the company store by the men on the train to bring them something back. They didn't have to come out for nothing. Most of them used tobacco, and they'd just order and have it brought up. You'd get your mail and everything delivered by the train when it came to camp."

DOCTORS

"They had a doctor over at Cass, and most of his business was for the men working for the company. He had some outside business, but not much. If a man got so bad they couldn't get him out, why they'd bring him (the doctor) in on a motorcar. He'd go in and doctor them, and then bring them in later.

"The train came out every day and if you was sick, you could get on it and come out to the doctor."

CARE OF TOOLS

"We always had a blacksmith at the camps. They shoed the horses, fixed grabs, about everything a blacksmith would do. They had a filer, a saw filer, to sharpen the saws, and he would generally file saws for about eight or nine crews. You'd pick out a saw in the morning, and you'd run that saw until noon. Then you'd bring it in at noon, and he'd have another one sharpened for the afternoon. About eight crews, that would be sixteen saws a day, that he took his flat files and sharpened. He worked down at the camp, but he would also come out into the woods to see how his saws were cutting. He'd correct them out in the woods if they needed it. He'd come out in the woods maybe once a week to check his saws.

"The crews would grind their own axes. Say, if I had you with me, we would grind our own axes. We had big grinding wheels that we turned by hand to grind the axes with. They had a bucket and all the time you were turning, the water would drip on the stone — all the time you were grinding. You can't grind on a dry stone."

YOUTH

"When I was young, I stayed with this old fellow for about thirteen years. He brought me up. When it was too bad to do any farm work, we would cut sprouts — use a scythe to cut sprouts. Where we were cutting sprouts at one time, there was tree stumps and some of them was six or seven feet off the ground. I thought to myself, them must have been the tallest men back in them days that I had ever seen. That old man was awful nice, but he never talked much. I said, 'How big was the men when you were a boy?' He said, 'Well, they were just the same as they are now.' I said, 'Well, they sawed them trees off there eight or ten feet, and I can't even reach up to where they sawed them off.' He said, 'When them trees was cut, this whole country was adrift with snow, and it froze. They stood right on the crust and cut them. Some of this country was six or seven feet deep with snow, and they pulled them logs right over top of that crust. You didn't know there was a fence down through there. That's how they cut them so high.' He also said, 'When they had these river drives, they sawed them way up high because the butt of them had all the resin in them, and they wouldn't float.' They was heavy, and it would sink the log. So they sawed them high to get above it. They cut them off about three feet above the ground. If you read the book, *Riders of the Flood* (by W.E. Blackhurst), every bit of that is true. Those old men have told me all of those things.

"Those old men would get right out on that river, when the logs would jam up, with a long pole and push and break them loose. It don't take much of a push in water. That's how they broke the jam. I guess several got drowned or crippled up.

"When you cut trees, you had to put them where you wanted them. If the tree was leaning down and your road was a little uphill, you couldn't cut that tree right straight across. You could notch that tree even if it was leaning, and then just stick you ax in it and sight your ax handle. You could generally pull them right wherever you wanted to pull 'em. They won't break off unless you get a brash one. Lots of times you would get a brash and dead one; they start to break. You could draw them as much as fifteen feet. If the tree was pretty straight, you didn't have to put much of a notch in them. If it was leaning the way that you was notching it, if you didn't put a good notch deep, just as soon as you got started to sawing, it would buck. The back side would start splitting off, and you'd ruin the whole tree. Just as soon as a tree would start busting up, you'd better leave

Cutting a tree — Picture loaned by Susan Monk.

her if it's a big tree. If it was a little tree, then sometimes you could hurry up and saw a little more; then you could save it. But most of the time when they started, they'd go fast. Go up there eight or ten feet and split off and jump back. They could go up the hill for ten feet or down the hill.

"I've had limbs to hit me or something like that—hit my eyes or something. I've had a lot of close calls, but I've never been really hurt. I was cut several times.

"If you worked for the company, the company furnished the saws. But, if you was cutting by the thousand and working for yourself, you furnished your own tools.

"A five and a half foot saw could cost you about five dollars. We used a Simmon saw. You could get more leverage on a bigger saw. If you've got the strength to pull them, you are all right. But, if you don't have the strength, then a short one is better for you.

"I could file a saw, back then, in about twenty/twenty-five minutes if it wasn't in too bad a shape. You only run them a half a day. If you rocked them or something and knocked some teeth off, you'd have to joint them.

"There was a feller over here by the name of Arbogast, and if you broke a tooth out, he would groove a new tooth on the saw for you. He'd groove each side and put a new tooth in it, and it would stay right there and never come out. Just groove it, like you was grooving a piece of wood. He was an extra good machinist.

"You could use a saw with a broken tooth, but it wouldn't cut right. There was a drag. Your cutting teeth cut it off, and your drag took it out—what your cutting teeth cut out. When you would come to this tooth, there wasn't a tooth there to cut; and when your drag would catch it and have to tear it out, you could feel it, grabbing and jerking it out. It would jump.

"If you kink one, it wasn't any count. You can't do anything with it once it has been kinked. They pull hard and rub against the side. They won't run through the groove right. If a saw is cutting right, the back of your saw will run the groove and hardly ever touch either side of the groove."

LOG DRIVES

"The log drives were before my day, but an old man told me that when they drove the logs to Ronceverte on the river, they didn't have a railroad then. They would build a dam out of logs, and then they skidded the logs out there and waited for the water to come up. When it got up enough to float them, then they'd just roll them in on each side, and then they knocked the dam loose. Then they followed the logs on foot, and they also had rafts built that they got on at night and to eat on. When dark came, they would just hook their raft up, anchor it to a tree, and go to bed. The next morning they'd go out and loosen the raft, and any logs that rolled out of the water, they'd roll them back in. They'd walk to Ronceverte and back home. He told me that they wore the old 'bib' overalls back in them days. He said that he had come out of the water many a time and his britches would freeze, and when he would go to do something, they would be froze so hard that they would break off. He wouldn't have nothing but knee britches on. I know the man wasn't lying. He said he'd seen a many a one do that.

"He said they have walked back from Ronceverte when the snow was up around his belt. he said Dave Smith, he was a tall and long-legged man, would break the trail for the rest of them in the snow when they would be walking back. There would be several with him, Ed Jackson, Blaine Knottingham, a Taylor down here, and others."

RIDING THE TRAIN

"The men would ride on the platform on each side of the engine going up the mountain on Sunday evening or down on Saturday. The hot water tank was in there, and it didn't matter how cold it was, the heat from the engine would keep you warm there. You would get your eyes and hair and everything full of cinders riding there. There was a rod that ran along there to hang on to. Ten or twelve men would ride on each side of the engine.

"Them old boxcars and log cars was cold to ride in during the winter. But, when you got on that platform around the engine, it would keep you warm. The sparks from the engines would cause fires every now and then. Most of the fires was down in the low section where the sod was. They'd get them out pretty quick.

"I was riding the train off of Cheat Mountain once. There was a boy that I knew that was a brakeman on that train. They called 'em, 'Jim Crow.' The old trains had a wheel, and they'd run a piece of iron with a hook on it through the bars and that would give you more power to turn the break wheels. The brakes was just steel against steel. They was hard to turn in.

"His 'Jim bar' broke, and he went down, and it just cut him up in pieces as big as your hand. There was a railroad switchback, and his

Yeager and Hoover Lumber Company Shay Number 1 — Loaned by Pocahontas Historical Society.

heart was laying in that switchboard — just cut him completely to pieces. When the bar broke, it just dropped him between the cars. I didn't think a man could be cut up that bad. That is the only train accident that I witnessed, and that was enough for me.

"Another time we was taking out bark. These hollers was steep where we were loading. One Sunday, they had these boxcars pushed to the head of the holler and had 'em set. The boss asked if we'd load 'em. They'd push them to the head of the holler with the train, and when you'd get a pile of two or three cord on, then all you had to do was release the brakes and ease them down the hill to the next pile and load it. Then when it was all loaded, the train would come and pick it up.

"We was up there and had them about half loaded, and it came a shower of rain. I told 'em, 'You start that thing this time, and it ain't gonna stop.' The boss said, 'We can stop her.' There was a track on top of those old boxcars to walk and a brake on the end to tighten with a wheel. Me and another boy was on top, and he told us to let it down to the next pile. We started it, and there was no stopping it. It was about fourteen feet from the top of it down to the ground. I said, 'You'd better jump.' There was a bunch of pine limbs cut there, and we jumped into that. That thing went right on to the switchback and over. It knocked a big birch tree down and went right on over in the holler. They didn't get nothing out of that car. The wheels was sliding on that wet track. It just slid like a sled. The further it went, the faster it went. When it went out of sight, it was going.

"There was a lot of boxcars wrecked, but I never knew of a train getting away. They had sand, they let out on the track when they'd start sliding. There was a lot of tons on behind them when they come off the mountain, but they kept that sandbox and you could tell when the wheels was sliding, and they'd put that sand on the tracks."

Bill Harper

by George Coury and Jeff Fife

We met Bill Harper, who has owned and worked on sawmills most of his life. Bill worked on the later mills, and compared earlier timber customs to those of today.

"My first experience working on a sawmill was between my junior and senior year in high school in 1929. Our home was in Buckhannon, and my father and a Mr. Bwiley operated a sawmill there. After October of 1929, the lumber business, like everything else, was real rough because in October is when the stock market crash occurred. It was almost impossible to sell any lumber. So we finished up that tract of timber in 1929.

"The next summer, the lumber was still piled there in the lumberyard. So, my father and mother and I went down and stayed in the old lumber camp. Dad and I trucked that lumber from the yard to the railroads.

"Practically all the lumber was shipped by rail at that time. We took part of it to Allendale which was near Camden on Gauley and part of it to Black Glenn down near Swiss. We could make about two trips a day by working a long day. The trucks then were much smaller and lighter and didn't haul the loads they do now.

"The two of us would load the trucks by hand. We would pick up each board. We didn't have forklifts then. Then we'd take the load to the railroad sighting and stack it off where it could be put into a boxcar whenever we were fortunate enough to receive an order.

"When I started in 1929, I started off bearing on the mill. That is taking the board from the saw and turning it down so that the bark edge would be up, and it goes from the off bearer to the edgerman. He can make the board without turning it over to edge it, cut off the bark edges.

"Sometimes you also had to take the slabs and run those out on the roller too. Sometimes these slabs were pretty thick and big. If the timber were big, you'd have a tree 24-36 inches and maybe crooked. A pretty good slab would come off it before you started taking the boards.

"It wasn't a particularly hard job, but I thought it would kill me. I recall the third day after I started to work. I was almost exhausted. I didn't think I could stand any more. Along about 10:30 A.M., the saw hit a pretty hard place in the log, and it made a ringing sound. Then the sawmills had a whistle; they were steam powered, and it had a steam whistle. Whenever they had to shut down for something, the sawman would give a little toot, or when we shut down for the evening, he tooted the whistle. When the saw hit that hard place, there was a ringing sound, and I turned to the edgerman and I said, 'Was that the whistle?' He looked at me in disbelief and said, 'No, that wasn't.' That afternoon I had to take off. I had someone else to take my place. But, I got to the place I could do it with one hand and enjoyed it. Of course, I just worked in the summer because I was in school.

"The next experience I had was hauling lumber over here in Pocahontas County in 1932. We were still living in Buckhannon, but Dad worked over here during the winter and sawed a contract for another lumber company. Another fellow and I trucked that lumber to Seabrick and stacked it up beside the railroad down there. I stayed at a farmhouse down near Mill Point, and we trucked that lumber.

"From there we moved to Jackson's River, Virginia, and Dad took a logging contract. It was a pretty tough proposition. We had to skid the logs down the mountain to a cliff, and then we'd dump them in the river and float them to a boom. Then we had to pull them out, load them and truck them to a little portable mill.

"They made the booms by chaining as many logs together as necessary and stretching them diagonally across the river so that they would feed to the side that you wanted them to come to. The chain wouldn't necessarily go clear across the river. They could use couplers. A coupler is a steel hook that has about a half a dozen links of chain, and then a swivel in the middle, and another hook. There is a hook on each end.

"They'd drive a coupler in a log and hook it to another log, and that way you could slide two at the same time. When you were going down a steep grade, the more logs you can pull, the more you hook together. All of the skidding was done with horses.

"One fellow's job was to drive grab; he was called a grab driver. He would make up the trail of logs by fastening them together with couplers. The teamster would frequently have to pull some of the logs out of the brush, or out to where the grab driver could get them, in order to make up a trail of logs. They put the larger logs in front and the smaller logs in the rear.

"Sometimes on a steep grade the logs would run on them. It would be so steep that they would move on their own, usually not on a hard road but on a wet or snowy road. The teamster would have to pull the team off to the side occasionally and let the logs run past. That was called 'jaying.' They had a special grab at the front of the rail so the team could 'jay.' It was simply a little snap that stuck up on a bar. And when they had to turn off sideways, it would open and let the logs go on down. If it didn't come loose as it was intended to do, why you was liable to cripple a horse."

FATHER'S BUSINESS

"Then my father and his partner, Mr. Curry, were in the lumber business for a number of years. Mr. Curry didn't take an active part in the lumber business, but he was more or less a silent partner. He had a general store in Marlinton, and he depended primarily for his profit from the operation to come from the trade he got from the employees of the mill. They traded at the store; whatever they bought was charged, and it would be taken off of their check in the lumber company office. They bought timber up near the trout hatchery. This was their first that they cut on their own, for themselves. They'd been cutting timber for the Jay Walker Wright Company of Bristol, Tennessee. From then on, they pretty much bought their own timber.

"In the fall of 1941, Dad was hunting over near the Virginia line and he was shot in the fleshy part of the back. The bullet stopped just short of the spinal column. This started Dad and Mr. Curry to thinking that if something happened to either of them, it would present a hardship—particularly to Mr. Curry, since he didn't know anything about operating a sawmill. So, they divided the assets of the company, and Dad was in business for himself.

"I had been teaching school in Buckhannon. I taught for six years. My wife and I were married while we were both teaching. So when school was out in 1941, I (was drafted) went to Fort Thomas. Then in late summer, they said anyone that was over twenty-eight years old could be released and transferred to the nearest reserve, if they wanted to be. Instead of going back to teaching, I come over here (to Pocahontas County). Dad said the war had caused quite a demand for lumber, and he was covered up. So, he said, 'Come over and go to work for me.' I worked with him for fifteen months and was called back into the service. When I came back from overseas, I went into the lumber business with my father. I worked then for eighteen years in the sawmill business at Mill Point. He had a large circular mill and a planing mill there. He bought lumber from them and sold it.

"I kept books, graded lumber, and worked as a part-time salesman traveling into southern Virginia and North Carolina. My father died in 1962. I sold the mill, but continued the brokerage business until 1970."

FIRING BOILER

"I remember one time we had a fire. Sawmills had a tendency, particularly when they were steam fired, to burn. You always had a fire hazard. You burned your refuge, slabs that you couldn't sell for firewood, and the sawdust.

"We burned that in the firebox under the boiler to heat the water. There was a conveyor that constantly carried the sawdust from the big saw, the main saw, to the hole in the top of what they called a Dutch oven. The oven was built of brick, and you used that sawdust as fuel. The mills that fired by steam had energy right there because of the waste from the mill.

"You used a blower with the sawdust, but once the fire gets going good and hot, you don't feed it too fast; it burns all right. Different species of wood burn at different rates.

"Ordinarily, they had a night watchman, and he would let the fire burn down at night. Then in the morning about an hour before the mill was supposed to start, he would build it up. You had to get the steam up. He'd get the steam up in time to start the mill. It was then the fireman's job to see that you had enough steam to run the mill.

"On your earlier mills, they used the slabs to fire with. They would hire somebody to run them out on a wheelbarrow on a track they would build and dump them off into the fire. That was a mean job. They were always heavier on one end than the other, and they are long. When you are trying to run them out on a wheelbarrow, they'd tip.

"Then later they had a slab conveyor. They were chains with the cleats on them. It carried them to a long trough and dumped part of the sawdust and the slabs into the fire.

"They have a chipper now. They grind the slabs into chips and take them to the paper plant. It has teeth on it something like an auger, and it just chews them up. As the chips are made, they are loaded directly on a truck; they used to load them on a boxcar on the train."

STEAM MILLS

"Most of the mills were steam mills. Later on, some of the mills converted to diesel power. Later, some of them operated, and still do, by electric power. A lot of changes has taken place in the lumber business. The forklift is a great advantage. They are able to forklift their logs, so they have all of one species together. They saw one species at a time. When they go to stack the lumber, that's a big advantage rather than have first an oak board, a cherry board, and a sugar board coming out because you have to put them in different stacks. Then when you load it, you can pick it up with a forklift and set it on the truck.

"They don't dry it in the lumberyards like they used to. It used to be, you couldn't hope to sell four quarter or inch oak until it had been on the stick for at least ninety days. Oak was one of the most difficult woods to dry. Some other woods dry faster. You can't dry oak too fast, or it will check on you. In other words, the surface would crack if the outside dries too quickly. These little cracks would go down into a board a considerable ways.

"In the summer when the sun would be hot on it, we'd gather up thin boards, miscuts, and cover the ends of the stacks to keep the sun from shining on it. I have seen people wet the boards when they'd be loading that lumber out, in order to close those checks, so it wouldn't be conspicuous to the next guy who might be inspecting it."

Mill at Widell, W. Va. — Loaned by Pocahontas Historical Society.

JOBS OF MILL

"When the logs came into the mill, they were dumped off the truck onto the skidways. There is generally two skidway men there. One washed the logs, and the other one rolled them down to the big saw. Some mills had live decks. They'd have chains that ran down to the sawmill on the skidway to carry the logs. That carried them down here without having to roll them. If they used steam to fire the mill, then the skidway men would use hot water with a lot of pressure on it to knock the ice, mud, and snow off the log, so it wouldn't dull the saw so quickly.

"The sawyer operated what they called the 'nigger.' That was the thing that pushed the log onto the carriage. You had a blocksetter that rode the carriage. Most larger mills had four headblocks (like standards on a truck). They were moveable. The blocksetter on the carriage could move them up. As he cut the board off, he worked the lever and pushed them up to saw the next board. The blocksetter had to know his business. The sawyer would signal to the blocksetter what he wanted him to set for; whether he wanted him to cut a five quarter (1¼") board, a four quarter board, or maybe it was a good looking face on the log and he wanted it cut thicker. The thicker lumber ordinarily was cut from the best part of the log; then you got down to the lower grade of lumber.

"Then there was the off bearer who turned the board down and

Bill Harper and MOUNTAIN TRACE Staff member, George Coury.

pushed it down the rollers a little ways and swings it over to the edgerman. The edgerman tips it off the rollers, sets his saw with a lever, and moves his saw right or left as he moves the handle. It is fed automatically through the edger. As the other end of the edger is the cutoff operator. Part of his job is picking strips. He has to take these edges that fall off the board; they actually come out on a big table; they don't fall off. He has to pick them up, tip them back onto the rollers or conveyor that carries them out to the fire or to the chipper, as it is now.

"Then they go to the trimmer, which has two saws. They can be adjusted by turning a crank, and they come closer together or farther apart. They trim the end off of the board square. When the timber cutters cut them, of course, they can't get them exactly square, and they ordinarily cut them a little long. Boards are ordinarily cut into even lengths, eight, ten, twelve, fourteen, or sixteen feet. A good timber cutter knows how much to allow for trimming. Once in a while someone will send some logs a little bit short, When that happens, you have to cut them back to the next shortest length.

"From the timber operator, they drop off onto another table for the green grader. The grade of a board may very well change as it dries. Defects may show up that didn't show up when it was green; also, the green grader doesn't have the time to grade accurately. He can't take the time to figure out it if will actually turn out to be a number one common, number two common, or whatever. A number two common, for example, will produce a fifty percent clear face in a certain number of pieces. A number two common is the surface measure divided by two. If it scales eight feet, that would be a board eight inches wide and twelve feet long; it would scale eight feet. You can have four pieces of that in order to get your fifty percent clear face. It is complicated. The green grader sorts it as best that he can in the time that he has. He then tips it into a little yard truck. Then it is run out to the stackers, two men, who put it on the stacks. Now, they've got the forklifts. They don't have elevated tracks that you did on the earlier mills. They have forklifts to pick the stuff up and run it down to the stacks."

DANGER

"A sawmill is a pretty dangerous place to work. You can hardly find a head sawyer; he has to adjust the saw guides which regulates the amount of tow to the logs that the big saw has. It is unusual to find a fellow who'd worked as a sawyer for many years and still have all of his fingers. We've had some pretty severe injuries at the mills."

BOILERS

"The boilers held a lot of water. I'd say a 45 horsepower boiler would probably hold a thousand gallons of water. It loses a lot of steam through exhaust.

"They have a water gauge on the front of the boiler. That shows you when your water is getting low, or if it's full. You don't let it get too low. If it happens to get out of sight on that gauge, then you are in trouble. If the water starts to get low, you open up the injector. It automatically puts water in. Steam runs through a line, and it has a check valve on it. The steam forces the injector to pick up water from the tank. You ordinarily have two or three tanks sitting around, from the well, to put into the boiler.

"Each time that piston works in a steam engine, there is an exhaust of steam that runs down your water. If it gets down too low, you are in grave danger of blowing up a boiler.

"If it would get too low, we would have to pull the fire — get a long rake that was kept there for that purpose and pull the fire from under the boiler. Over at French Creek, I saw a sight where a sawmill boiler had blown up. It was a pretty terrific explosion."

SMALL CIRCULAR MILLS

"The small circular mills used to be moved from one hollow to the next. If they had a considerable boundary of timber, they might just move a quarter of a mile. After they cut all of this hollow and everything skidded pretty easily to that mill, and they got that hollow cut out, then they'd move it down to the next hollow and skid that hollow out. In the course of a mile, they might have four or five different sets as it was called. There wasn't much to these mills, a head saw, perhaps a cut off, and maybe a little side edger."

TEAMSTERS

"The teamsters of the old mill era were sometimes referred to vulgarly as "horse drivers," and were the elite of the woods crew. They had to be men of cool judgment and even temperament. They directed the work of the grab drivers and the road monkeys. In my experience, the best teamsters were men who wasted few words and spoke quietly to both men and horses. They invariably developed a respect, if not affection, for the teams that they drove. They soon learned their team's limitations and did not call on them to exceed those limits. At the same time, they were quick to recognize a shirking horse and motivated the animal as required. The teamster took pride in his team, saw to it that they was properly fed, watered, groomed, and shod. He doctored their minor cuts, bruises, and colic, and kept the harnesses in good repair.

"Logging teams were special. They lived with danger and even the best of them sometimes were killed or disabled in their work. They started with intelligence and strength and, under the care of an understanding and experienced teamster, learned to do their job and avoid injury. They knew when the log trail they were pulling started to run on its own and how to get out of the way of the logs by running ahead or turning off into prepared 'jay holes' along the skid road. They recognized the voice of their driver and understood what he was asking them to do. The horses of a team were not merely compatible; they appeared to be dependent on each other, even on those rare instances when they were turned out to pasture where they stayed within a few feet of each other.

"Tracked tractors and rubber tired skidders now do the horses' work, but they cannot really replace them. For many of us, the disappearance of the teams and the teamsters from the logging woods ended a romantic era."

ALLEN BURGESS, LOGGER

"One, Mr. Allen Burgess, was the most colorful logger I knew. Allen 'Fuzzy' Burgess was not acquainted with his father, nor did I know anybody who was. Allen and I walked these mountains of Pocahontas County together looking at timber my father was considering buying. We often sat and talked while eating our lunches, 'catching our wind,' or comparing opinions of the timber we were seeing. He was the teacher, I, the pupil. Allen had no formal forestry training, but he had, probably of necessity, gone to work in the woods when he was fourteen years old. He told me of having worked in the thick stands of spruce on the mountaintops where, when the trees were felled and cut into logs, a man could literally walk on the logs for hundreds of yards without touching the ground.

"Allen was short, about five feet three. His feet and hands were small; his body was thick and strong; his eyes were blue, and his nose was short and sharp. His rare attempts to comb his short blond hair was invariable failures—the obvious roots of the nickname he endured but did not appreciate. In deference more to his temper than to his preference, Allen was referred to as 'Fuzzy' far more often in his absence than in his presence. His voice was high pitched, and his laugh matched. Every man who ever worked with him seemed to have a story based on exhibitions of Allen's hair-trigger temper. When on the job, he wore only typical logger garb: a good grade of calked leather cutters (special ordered because they were so small and in small demand in later years), 'Ritchie' underwear, shirt, and pants. His pants would be rolled or cut off halfway between his ankles and knees, and in warm weather, his shirt sleeves would be rolled halfway to his elbows exposing his long underwear from there to his wrist. He wore a faded felt hat creased crossways, in the manner of bona fide loggers. The hat brim was never turned down, and the tail of the Woolrich shirt was never tucked in, causing him to appear even shorter than he was.

"Taught only by experience and observation, Allen Burgess knew his trade as well as any man I ever knew. He could file a crosscut saw so skillfully that, in the hands of experienced log cutters, it would almost appear to drop through the trunk of a soft textured tree. He was a good axman and could cut a tree to fall where he wanted it to fall. He told me, 'Never buy an ax with red paint on it—they are no good.' He knew a host of clues that enabled him to tell a good tree from an unsound one. He 'swamped' the easiest routes for the skid roads. He built log skidways or landings that were solid, of correct height and slope for easy loading of the logs onto the trucks. At a glance, he could tell which side would be the 'run' of the log and where to drive the grab. These and hundreds of other things about logging were so practiced that for him, they were automatic.

"Allen eventually became our woods foreman; however, the first work he did for us was by the day with an old gray horse that he owned. He was *not* a good teamster. The arrangement was for him to use the horse to skid logs to a landing. The horse must not have been especially good at its part of the job for Allen was constantly yelling at it and frequently whipping it with first one thing or another—sometimes the cant hook. The horse thought very little of Mr. Burgess in return and, at every good opportunity, would bite him. While a horse has no fangs, he does have good strong teeth and jaws with which he can deliver a very painful wound. Allen would fly into a temper tantrum and whip the horse, unless prevented from doing so by other workers in the vicinity who often took the side of the horse. Allen would then jerk off his felt hat, throw it on the ground and jump on in with those calked shoes. The calks, more numerous and sharper than the spikes on golf shoes, would do absolutely nothing to enhance the value of the hat.

"On other occasions when Allen would be accidentally scratched, cut or bruised in his work, which can be fairly often in woods work, he has been known to throw his ax, saw, hammer, wedges, and his hat as far as he could into the brush as he cussed the inanimate object that contributed to his misery. On at least one instance, unawed by the spectacle of Allen's tantrum, a fellow worker cut a hickory switch and ordered Allen to go into the brush and collect his tools or suffer the indignity of having his pants cut off by the switch. The choice was not a difficult one.

"At another time, before everybody had an automobile and drove to and from work each day, we had moved a portable woods camp to the woods for some of the loggers who wished to stay on the job. Of course, there was a kitchen shack too. For some reason, the fellow who had been doing the cooking had to be gone for a few days. The other woodsmen finally prevailed on Allen to do the cooking until the regular cook could return to duty. Allen agreed to try it only on the terms that the first fellow who should complain about the cooking would automatically replace him.

"For supper Allen prepared a batch of 'logger' beans. The men, a small crew, filed into the cook shack, filled their plates, and set to. One fellow put a huge spoonful of beans into his mouth, gasped, gulped some coffee, and croaked, 'Migawd, them beans are salty!' Quick as a wink, Allen was standing over him menacingly. The bean eater, realizing the position in which he had put himself, turned to Allen and said, 'But that's just the way I like 'em.'

"Allen mellowed with the passing years. He was always a hard worker and was liked and respected by the other men. He was a good woods foreman and saw to it that he and his men did their part to keep the operation going.

"Allen was an emotional man. Long after my father was gone Allen and I both retired from the lumber business, we often met and spoke of the earlier times. I discovered that I had to keep those conversations light and short lest Allen embarrass both of us by breaking into tears. He too is gone now, but I think some note should be made of him and his life, for he was surely one of a kind."

Markwood Gum
by Nancy Dykoff and Brian Davis

"I started to work in the timber industry when I was fourteen years old. That was in 1913, and I went to work for the Deer Creek Lumber Company.

"The Stepzinger's were the owners of the company, Elmer and Clyde. They were from Pennsylvania.

"I started driving team for them. That was all I ever done for them. I didn't do any cuttin' timber for them or anything like that. The Stepzingers contracted most of the cuttin' of the timber. They hardly ever cut any themselves; that is, the company did. They had six teams when I went to work.

"I was very small when I went to work for them. The boss took me to the barn and showed me the team. I had to get a box so I could put the harness on, but I got along all right. I knew how to put the harness on because we always had a smaller horse at home. They was the same kind of harness too.

"That winter the snow was about a foot deep when I went to work. They was skidding timber uphill with a block and chains. They couldn't get the railroad into the side of the mountain, so they skid the timber up and down the other side where the train track was. That was mostly

Captain Markwood Gum

We met Markwood Gum and learned of life in the lumber camps. After going to work at the lumber camps at the age of fourteen, he stayed there until 1918 when he went to Cass to work in the lumber mill until his retirement.

all I done that winter. It was a lot of work, but you take the snow on, and it would skid along pretty lively. Of course, some of it was terrible large timber. So much of it was chestnut trees back in that time; why, I couldn't see over the center of the logs. They called Big Ridge where we was skidding. It was mostly all hardwood. It was virgin forest then; it had never been cut before. I worked for them until 1918, the fall of 1918.

"I left there and went up to North Fork. I didn't stay there long though; that was too rough a country. The boss, Charlie Rossburg, I worked for at the sawmill up at North Fork was a regular horse killer. He wanted you to haul this one and that one, haul this one and that one. I told him when he asked me to take the team, I said, 'I'll do the load-

Ready to start cutting — Picture loaned by Susan Monk.

ing, not you.' I said, 'If that don't suit you, I'll not take them.' That was all there was said.

"The horses had to be shod. In the wintertime they had sharp toes and corks so they wouldn't slide around. Of course, in the summertime, the shoes were just square. If you pull a shoe off, you quit right there and take them to the blacksmith shop and get it put back on. Sometimes, they would over-reach or something and pull a shoe. You don't pull a horse that don't have a shoe on.

"The blacksmith also took care of all the repairs. If you broke any grabs or couplers or anything like that, he would put new links in them, weld them together, put new cant hook handles in, just anything that had to be done.

"When I worked for the Deer Creek Lumber Company, it was mostly hardwood, and they peeled it. Then in the spring after they brought the logs off, they brought the bark off. We hauled the bark on sleds down to where the railroads was and loaded it into box cars. Then they took it up to the tannery.

"I went to work for the North Fork Company. The mountain was very rough, steep, and rocky. I drove team there until July 1, 1919. One of the horses I drove was getting real hot, and if you gave him lots of water, he'd get sick. I took two or three days off, and when I went back down, why he had passed away. The boss told me to take another old horse up with the good horse. I told him no. I didn't want to take that crippled horse out, he'd just get killed. He said, 'He wasn't no good anyway.' I didn't like the idea, but I took him out Monday morning and went to the top of the mountain and got a trail made up. I think we had about twenty-eight logs, and we grabbed on the haul—it didn't move. I just unhooked 'em, drove 'em out, tied 'em up and walked back over the mountain. I met the grab driver coming down to see what the trouble was. I told him, whenever the boss comes up, I said, 'You tell him to take the team down the mountain that I didn't want to kill old Fred.' He came up, and he told him, and sure enough that is what happened.

"I didn't even go towards the camp. I came across this side and walked to Arbovale and caught the mail hack and went to Cass. I went to work at Cass Lumber Yard at noon. So, I was at Cass until 1960, the first of July, forty-one years. While I was at Cass, I was piling and grading lumber, either in the mill or out in the yard."

LOG TRAIL

"They had couplers that they put the logs together with. The grab had three lengths and then a swivel in the middle and three lengths on the other end. Unless you had a powerful big log, they would leave at least six or eight inches (between the logs). They generally tried to get a large log to start down the mountain. When we started off the mountain, we never brought them all the way to the landing; we'd have to turn them loose. When the spreaders started hitting the horse's heel, you couldn't hold them ahead of the trail of logs at all. They knew to jay and let the logs go. They knew to get out of the way. When the horses jayed, the spreader hook would come unhooked from the front grab and the logs would go on. The team would be at the side. Whenever a team got used to getting out of the way, you couldn't hold them. If it didn't come unhooked, they'd take the head log right out in the woods with them. That's what they called 'jack pottin'.' The logs would just pile up all over the place, and you'd have to tear them all apart. I've hauled as many as thirty logs at once. The biggest job was getting them out into the road and getting them hooked together. It wasn't hard pulling, going down.

"After the logs slid off the mountain to the landing, they generally had a place dug out to stop the logs. Then, they rolled them over the hill where the railroad was.

"Then they had loaders that would load the logs on the cars of the trains. The train cars had bunks on them, just like your trucks nowadays, that hauled the logs. That's the way the railroad cars was, and they'd be different lengths. At Cass they used solid cars thirty-two feet long. But, the ones that come up here were sixteen feet long. They cut their timber longer over there. Sometimes they would put longer logs on a car, and they'd reach back to the next car. So then, they would have to put shorter logs on the next car. That would give them a chance to get long pieces in. Then, they could cut whatever length they wanted in the mill.

"When they got to the mill, they dumped the logs into a pond. The logs would then float over and would be drawn with big chains, what's called a 'jack smith.' With it got into the mill, they'd have a ruler there and measure the size of the log; and if it was big enough to make whatever the order was, they'd made it whatever length they wanted it.

"I never saw any spruce that was too big. I have saw them make 12 x

Crane loading the log train — Loaned by Pocahontas Historical Society.

12's out of spruce. Now take hemlock, you can make a 24 x 24. It was so much larger. It came off Elk, down next to Snowshoe, what's called Slady Fork.

"The train made two trips to Bald Knob a day, one in the morning and one in the evening when they was hauling logs. If they had to go clear into Slady Fork and get the logs, they only made one trip a day. See then, they had to go to Slady Fork and bring them up to Spruce and then down to Cass. Of course, the big engines always made that long trip. They could haul thirteen cars. The little engines could only haul six. The ones that they use for the tourist trains today are the ones that could only haul six cars. They had one, Number Twelve, that was the biggest engine in the world over at Cass.

"If the trains got to pulling hard and started to slipping, then they had to put water on the tracks and sand with it. So, they had to put a longer water tank on, built it longer. That's what made it the largest engine in the world. Then, they (West Virginia Pulp and Paper Company) bought two other engines, Numbers Thirteen and Fourteen. They was long, but not as large as Number Twelve.

"They could take around twenty-five or thirty spruce trees at once. Now, if you take the hardwood that was kind of crooked, you couldn't get that many on.

"They put four stakes on each side of the train car. Then they put four chains on each car. They had them fixed where they could knock them chains loose on the one side where they dumped them in the pond. Then they had to chop the stakes on the other side, so when they knocked the chains loose they would break. Then, they had to put four new stakes in that side of the car every time they went to the woods. The chains went across the top of the logs and fastened to stakes on the opposite side. Then, they would put some logs on top of that to hold them down. The chains were just made long enough to go across the car. Then, they used a long handled hammer to knock them loose on the one side of the car when they were ready to unload them. Then when the logs came off, the chains still stayed hooked to the opposite side.

"Your hardwoods are not as tall as the spruce or hemlock. They are also more crooked. You take spruce and hemlock. On the average, they are pretty straight. But, you take hemlock, it gets shaky. When you chop it up into lumber and it dries, it's not solid. It's like the wind had been kicking it.

"There is poplar and cucumber. Most people puts it into what they call poplar. But, it is two different kinds of wood. It's the same color, but it is a different kind of wood. The cucumber is a harder wood than the poplar, what's called yellow poplar. Also, the hard maple is a tougher wood than the soft maple. There is two kinds of maple, too. If you was ever around wood, you could see the difference. It wouldn't take you long to learn it.

"Red oak is a much better lumber than the other kind of oak. White oak is tougher than red oak, but you hardly ever get a good tree. It has little spots on it. I don't know what causes it, something stinging it when it's growing or what. Red oak, just holds the same color all of the time, and it is much better for any kind of building purposes."

CREWS

"They had what you call timber cutting crews. They had buck swampers. They went along and looked the place over and decided where to make the roads, where they could get the most timber to these roads. That was the first men in, the swampers. Then the cutting crews cut the timber down and cut the logs up according to the orders; that is, if the trees were good enough and straight enough to make it. You've got to cut a lot of short logs to get rid of a crooked area. In the hardwood, they can cut lots of short stuff into lumber. Now you take that spruce and things like that, you can get a good sixteen foot in logs easily, sometimes a couple of them. We just left the limbs and tops lay. It don't take very long for them to rot. Two or three years and they won't even make firewood.

"We used a crosscut saw. It took two men to use it. They were about six foot long. They also had a man to do the notching, called fitters, He also did the measuring too. Then they had a knot bumper. He was the one who cut the limbs off, unless they were large limbs. Then they cut them with the saw. They had a saw filer to sharpen the axes and saws. They had a cook at each camp. Then they had a helper called cookee. The cooks had to get up around four o'clock in the morning to start. They did a lot of their work the night before. They would have a regular meal for breakfast. They would have potatoes, eggs, meat, and biscuits."

FIRST STARTED

"When I first went to work, I got 20 cents an hour, ten hours a day. That was $2.00 a day. We generally started to work around 6:00 A.M. to 6:30 P.M. We stayed in camps, and they had cabins to stay in. They had them fixed so when the timber ran out and they needed to move, you could put a cable around them and take the loader that they loaded logs with and just lift them up and set them on a railroad car; then they'd take them to the next camp, and set them up. They moved them by train, when it was time to move. Barns for the horses were moved the same way.

"They were just a box, a box cabin. There wasn't much furniture. There was plenty of gray backs, bedbugs and everything else. They had the cabins fixed so that they set together. You could just go from one to another. Sometimes not many stayed at camps because a lot of people working would stay at home. It was just mainly the ones that drove team that stayed in the camps.

"There was even one fellow that drove team that went home. He had asthma awful bad. He couldn't lay down to sleep. He had to sit up to sleep. The rest of us fellows would take care of his team too.

"The first camp that I was at, the boss's wife done the cooking. It was unusual for a woman to cook in the camps. The food was good as I was used to, plenty of potatoes, beans, applesauce and everything like that. We had 'logger berries.' Prunes, you know, we called them 'log-

Lumbering camp — Picture loaned by Susan Monk.

ger berries.' Up at North Fork, nearly everybody stayed at the camp up there 'cause it was too far away from home.

"I never played cards. We weren't allowed to play poker at the camps. But on Sundays, they'd slip out in the woods and play, if the weather wasn't bad. I usually went home on the weekends, went back on Sunday evening. The ones that wanted to leave, they'd have someone to take care of the horses on Sunday for them. If the train hadn't left with their load of logs, we rode the train down, so we didn't have to walk. Sometimes, I would just as soon walk. It really was rough riding. I never knew of a train running away up at North Fork, but they did over at Cass."

SLIDING LOGS

"They slid the logs off the mountain on dirt. One place where I worked and where the logs came off the mountain, there was a run. They had to pole that run to keep it from digging so deep. They zigzagged the poles, put one log one way and the other across the other way. This was to keep the logs in the center of the poles and to

Timber crew — Picture loaned by Susan Monk.

keep from cutting the run down too deep. After they got the poles over and the water running over it, it made it easier to skid. Them horses knew right where to step all of the time crossing this. The horses would take care of themselves if you just gave them a chance. Of course, nobody was going to contrary them very much after knowing them and knowing what they was going through with.

"They used mostly Percheron and Clydesdale horses. It seemed like the Belgians were more clumsy. They had so much more hair on their legs down around their hocks, and they'd get mud, and they had more trouble with them with scratches and one thing and another like that. I don't think I ever saw any mules used except when I was little. When I was about six or seven years old, over on the Holsterman line, they had one pair of mules. Them mules knew more about skiddin' than most people do. Half of the time the man driving them didn't have a line on them. He'd hang the lines up on the hames. He'd just talk to them.

"When you took the horses in of a night after a day's work, you had to curry them, wipe the sweat off them, doctor any scratches or cuts that they got, give them plenty of bedding, and feed them."

Cass, A Lumber Town
by Joan Carte

As our contacts reminisced about their days in the lumber camps and their work in the lumber mills, we asked each one about Cass, the largest lumber mill and town in West Virginia in its day. The following is a combination of their thoughts which describes the town of Cass. Cass is now owned and operated by the state of West Virginia, and one may go there and ride the old Shay engine to the top of Cheat Mountain. We hope that after reading the lumber stories, you will want to visit this historic town and spend a few hours.

"All of these houses at Cass belonged to the company. There was a church in the middle of them, and I would say the company built it too. The company owned all of the land on its side of the river. As you drive into Cass today, the houses and buildings before you cross the river were owned by local people raised there. The company didn't allow saloons on their side of the river, so they were all located on the side of the private houses. They had fights and squabbles.

"When the company was there, they kept their side pretty well policed. From the time I worked there, your time was kept on Cheat Mountain. They couldn't pay you up on Cheat, you had to come off to the office at Cass and get your money. You could take your check right into the company store, and they'd cash them. They didn't pay in scrip at Cass.

"These old men that didn't come off the mountain for months could send in to the company store and get things, and they would just

Town of Cass

charge it to them. Then when they come to get their check, they would deduct the charges (at the store) from the check they got.

"When they ran the train and the camps on the mountain, they had that big company store full of everything. The upstairs was full of beds and furniture and anything that you wanted. It was three stories tall. Anything that you wanted to buy, that store had. In below, they had 'tater' bins. I don't know how many hundreds of bushels of 'taters' they'd have down there. They furnished the mountain (sawmill camps) with all the 'taters,' meats, and stuff like that. They had meat cutters in there and everything. It was an up-to-date store for its time.

"The company owned their own operation (log camps and mill), and you take harness, grabs, cant hooks and saws; and if you are running several camps, those supplies fill up a lot of room. So, they had all three stories pretty well filled with supplies. When you needed something like that at camp, you'd just send down by the train, and they'd bring it back up.

"They did have a post office in part of the downstairs of the store, but everything else was store connected.

"The old hotel was over on the corner before you crossed the bridge. They called it the White Elephant, I believe. There was four or five other places there where the timbermen would stay when they come off too. They sold whiskey and beer, and they'd get them drunk and maybe steal half of their money before they would get away. There was different places you could buy whiskey and stay.

"They had a jail over there. I think it would only keep four or five. It wasn't big enough for too many. I've seen 'em slap four or five in there when they'd get drunk.

"They kept a night watchman at the mill, in the store and places like that, where they needed them. They had the whole town protected well.

Front St., Cass, W. Va.—Picture loaned by Pocahontas Historical Society.

"Cass was the biggest operation around. Raywood was next to it. That was below Cass, about ten or twelve miles. That's all tore up and gone now. But, there was lots of houses there at one time, but not as many as they had at Cass. Private people bought the land up, down there.

"The company houses at Cass, where the working men lived, had a kitchen, dining room, and living room downstairs and a couple of bedrooms upstairs. They were all built about alike. Most of the men that lived in them worked in the mill or at the shops. There was some men that worked on the mountain that lived in these houses though. They stayed on the mountain during the week and come off every weekend to be with their families. The railroad crew also lived in these houses.

"After you got on up on the mountain where the store owners, supervisors, doctors and the higher-ups lived, they were big houses.

They was build well and furnished well too. They were on the road where you started up Back Mountain.

"They didn't have streets through the town. They had boardwalks. A boardwalk down in front of the houses, and then each house had a boardwalk that came out and joined the main one. Whenever a board would get bad, the company had a crew that would put in a new one, and, if needed, put in a new section of walk. They kept it up good until after the company went out.

"At Cass they also had a foundry to make broken pieces of machinery. They'd take the broken piece out and set it in sand, put it together, and make a mold in sand. Then they'd take the piece out of there very carefully, not to disturb the sand. Then they'd melt the iron and pour it in the sand to make the broken piece."

arts & crafts

The Art of Teneriffe Embroidery
by Lisa Farrah and Jane Shepherd

Teneriffe Embroidery gets its name from Teneriffe lace which closely resembles it in looks and technique. Teneriffe lace was woven in blocks on a small frame and fastened together in designs to form doilies. The work, as we know it, has the appearance of drawn work, but the motifs are woven on top of the fabric. Since they are square, they are easily done in checked gingham; however, this is not a necessity.

This craft is suitable for cushions, wall hangings, place mats, luncheon cloths, dresses, curtains, etc.

The name "Teneriffe" indicates that the craft originated on the island of Teneriffe off the coast of Spain. We have found a number of older women of different nationalities who have known the craft since childhood.

Mrs. Elizabeth Harbert first brought Teneriffe embroidery to Salem, West Virginia. She taught this craft to Ireta Randolph, who later taught Shelba Zirkle. Shelba, an instructor at Fort New Salem, shared the following instructions with our readers.

TENERIFFE or "GINGHAM EMBROIDERY" is made of two distinct patterns. It is outlined by a seven block square of ¼" checked gingham. Double cross-stitch is used on dark squares and single cross-stitch on alternate squares.

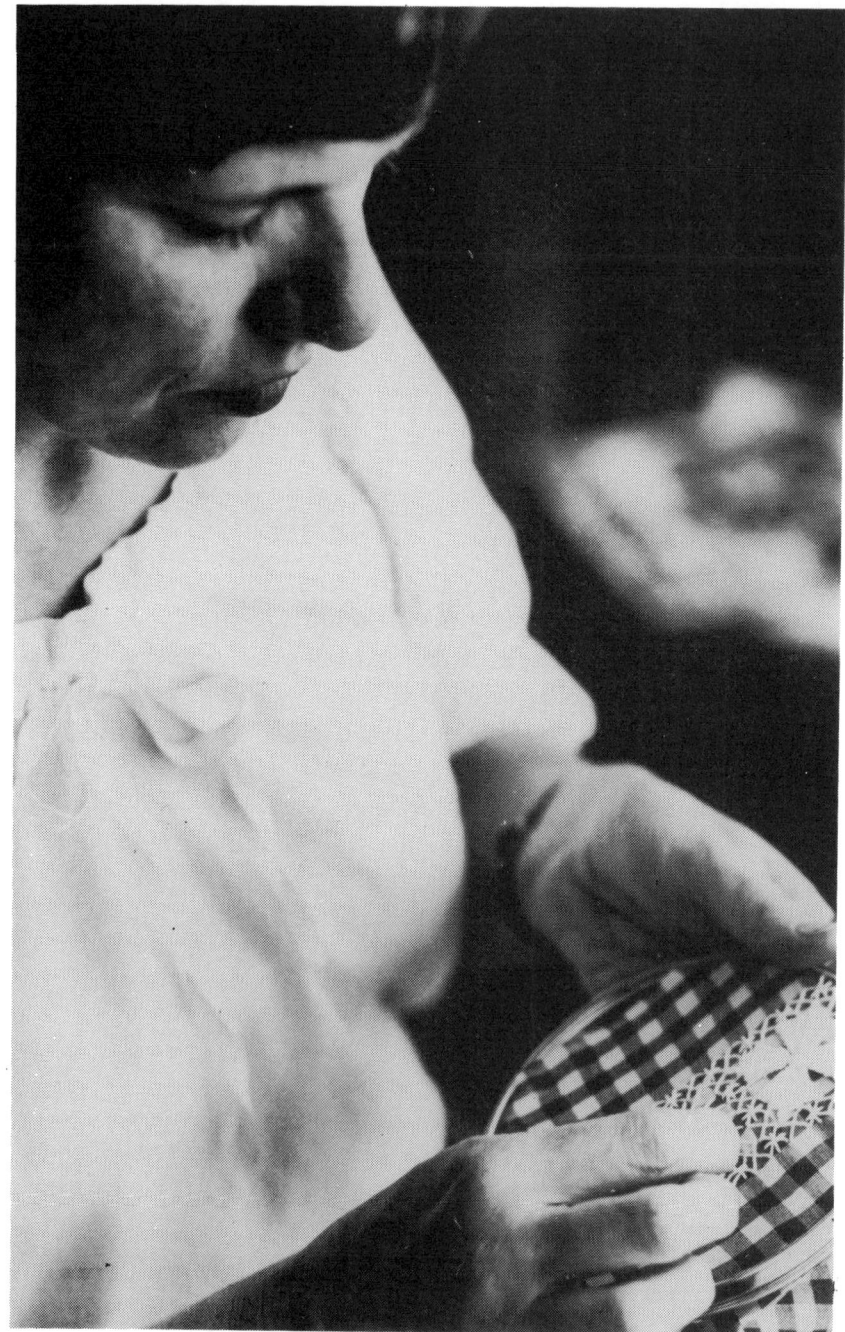

Shelba Zirkle demonstrates tenneriffe embroidery.

no. 1

no. 2

For No. 1, start at any point and work to the opposite point, making a large double cross-stitch in the center. Separate into four even sections and bring the needle from back of the material into the center square. Make a cross-stitch to hold the web firmly in the center.

To weave, bring the needle out between any two threads of the web near the center. Slip the needle (eye end first) under two web threads each time, as shown. This forms a back stitch. Continue to work around until the web is filled.

No. 2 pattern is made in the same manner as the weaving point.

To weave — bring the needle out where the web stitches converge.

Using eye end of the needle, go under three threads of the web as shown. Turn and go under remaining two threads. Continue weaving until the outside threads are filled. Drop to the three remaining threads and weave in the same manner until they are filled. The center thread is filled by looping thread around it four or five times filling it to the corner.

The three remaining sections are done as described above.

Different designs can be obtained by placing these patterns in a variety of arrangements.

A variation of cross-stitch can be very helpful to tie designs together.

MATERIALS NEEDED:

¼ inch checked gingham of a variety where the blocks are completely square — I recommend DAN RIVER BRAND.

Thread — I use SOUTH MAID BRAND, mercerized; it has a hard twist and works very well. The DMC COTTON PERLE -5 BRAND. is especially good but is difficult to get locally. You could use J. & P. COATS "KNIT-CRO-SHEEN" which has an excellent sheen, but frays easily.

Embroidery hoop, embroidery needle,

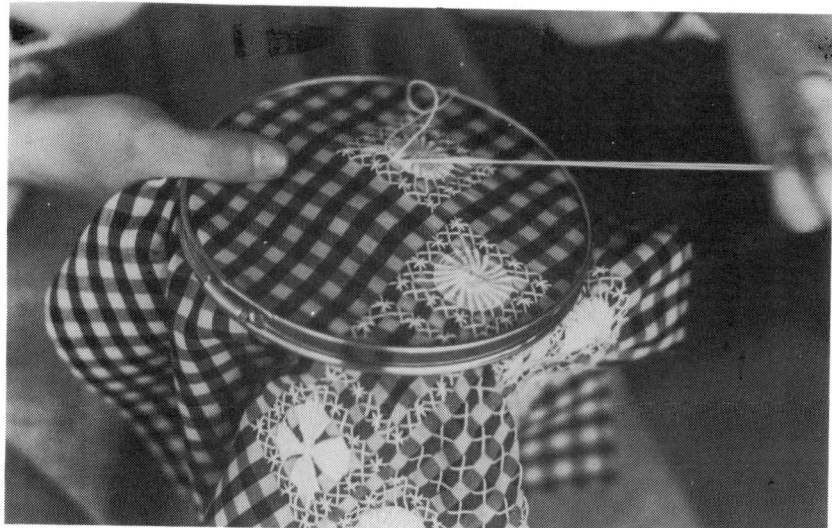

Close up look at tennerriffe embroidery.

Rug Braiding
by Bari Marshall

While we were visiting the fort to learn of the art of Teneriffe embroidery, Shelba Zirkle also shared the art of rug braiding with us.

To start braiding, you take three strips of cloth about two inches wide (length can vary).

Put the strips of cloth on top of each other and use a clothespin to hold them together. Then you put a string through the hole of the clothespin. This string and clothespin will serve as a hanger to hold the strips when you start braiding. You can then tie the braids to a doorknob or a nail or a wall.

Before you start braiding, fold the edges of each strip of cloth over about one quarter of an inch. Keep the edges of all the strands folded in while you braid.

To braid, take the right strand and fold it over the middle. The middle strand then becomes the right strand. Then fold the left strand over the middle one. The left strand becomes the middle one. Keep repeating the basic process until you get to the end of the strips.

When you come to the end, sew it to keep it from unbraiding. As you start making the rug, overlap the braids about one half inch and sew them together.

Lay the braids on a table and start turning them in a circular fashion to create the rug.

Keep the braids lying flat on the table, and sew them together on the bottom so you can't see the seam when it is finished.

Keep the braids going in a circular pattern until the rug is finished. You must keep the rug flat when you are sewing so it will not get bulges in it.

The size of the rectangular rug depends on the size of the first braid. Subtract the width of the rug from the length to get the size. For a 9' x 12' rug, the length of the first braid would be three foot long; a 3' x 5' rug would be two feet long.

To finish the rug, just taper your strips by cutting them different widths about 18" from the end.

BRAIDED RUGS

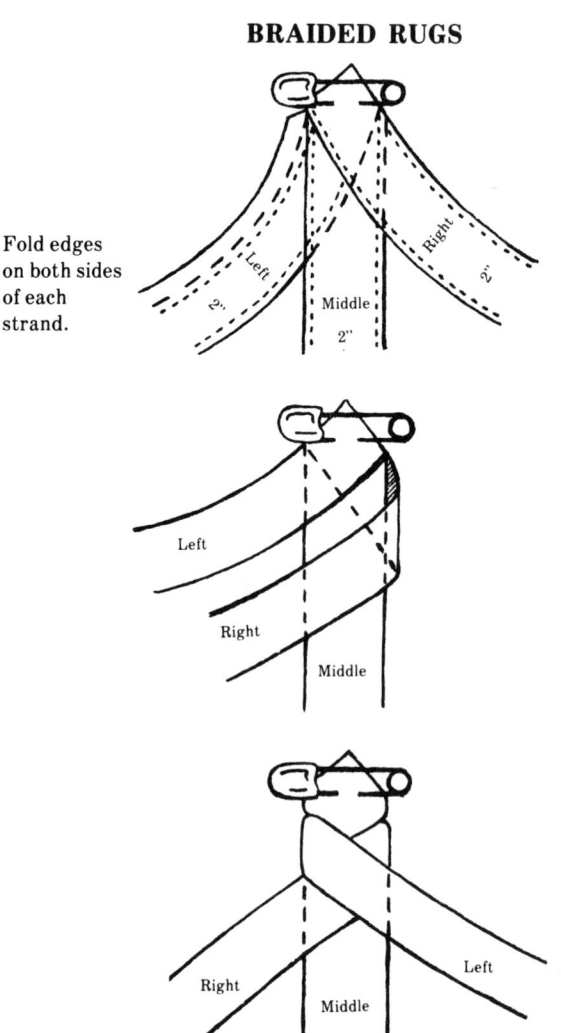

Fold edges on both sides of each strand.

Playing The Dulcimer
by Carolyn Schwab

Dr. Patrick Gainer, Professor Emeritus of West Virginia University, was for many years a collector of the folklore and music of West Virginia.

After finding the dulcimer maker, we contacted Dr. Gainer and asked his assistance in preparing an article on playing the instrument. The following article was written by Dr. Gainer and includes a song from his collection, as formerly sung by Aunt Mary Wilson of Gilmer County.

THREE-STRINGED DULCIMER

The instrument, which is commonly called the dulcimer today, is probably a descendant of the Arabic rebec, which was brought to England. The rebec was a popular folk instrument in England in the seventeenth century. John Milton describes the village dancers dancing to the music of the "jocund rebec," in his poem **L'Allegro.** The instrument, or at least the knowledge of how to make it, was brought to America by the early settlers. It has not been well-known in the Appalachian mountains until it was heard at folk festivals after 1950. Since then, it has become very popular, and numerous craftsmen have become dulcimer makers.

Dr. Patrick Gainer lectures to MOUNTAIN TRACE Staff about folk music of West Virginia.

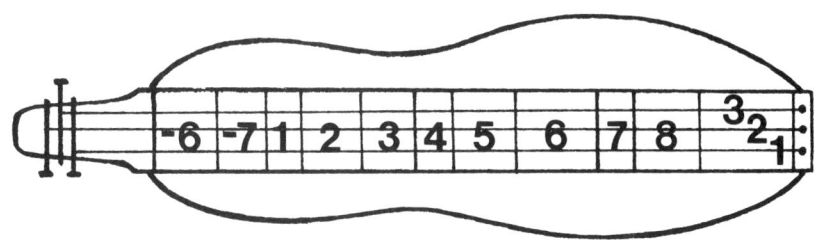

Tune string number 1 in C
Tune string number 2 in C
Tune string number 3 in F

WHAT SHALL I GIVE TO THEE?

Collected by Patrick W. Gainer
as sung by Aunt Mary Wilson
of Gilmer County.

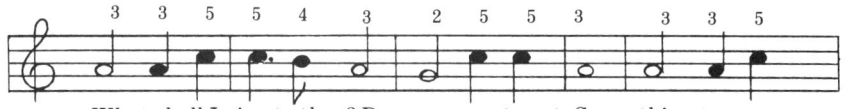

What shall I give to thee? Dear, we must part, Some-thing to
What shall I give to thee? Life is so strange, All I could

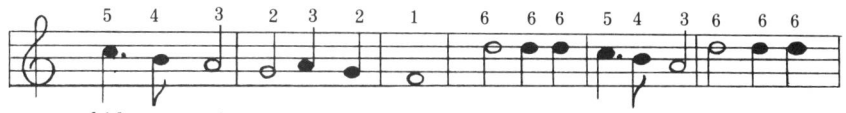

hide a-way close to the heart. Give me an i-vy leaf, Fresh from the
of-er thee sure-ly must change.

vine, Give me an i-vy leaf, Green as the pine.

TO PLAY THE DULCIMER

Most players place the instrument on the lap, but some prefer to place it on a table to play it. It is played by sliding a small wooden stick, called a "noter," up and down the first string only, while striking all three strings with a pick — a celluloid collar stay or a turkey quill.

Hold the noter in the left hand and press it down firmly on string number 1 on the fret indicated by the number to sound the note needed for the melody of the song. Then you strike all three strings with the pick; you will thus hear the melody note on string number 1, while strings 2 and 3 will sound drone notes. Be sure to fret only string number 1, and do not touch the other strings with the noter. Strings number 2 and 3 will remain constant in tone through the song, while string number 1 plays the melody. In order to prevent the noter from touching string number 2, hold the noter between the thumb and forefinger, using the forefinger as a guide.

In earlier times the instrument was often played with a bow which looked much like the kind of bow that is used for shooting arrows. The bow was applied to all three strings at the same time, thus keeping the drones playing constantly along with the melody.

Making The Dulcimer
by Ryan Swisher and Kelly Riel

To learn the art of dulcimer making, we contacted Tom Dailey and Alvin Moore. Mr. Dailey talked with us about the preparation and construction of the dulcimer, while Mr. Moore shared the methods of constructing and playing the hammered dulcimer.

"I've heard a lot of different views on the history of the dulcimer. The view that sounds the most logical and reasonable is that it originated strictly in the southern Appalachian region, and that it is an American instrument. But, when you see the examples of the European instruments that are basically the same, then it appears that it was carried over as an idea from Europe. I think the theory stands up pretty well. In France it is called the 'Emponete,' but a similar instrument in Germany is called 'Scheitholt.' Of course, you have mention of a dulcimer in the third chapter of the book of *Daniel*, in the *Bible*. That, I imagine, was something like the hammered dulcimer we know today.

"I talked to an old man from North Carolina that had an instrument that very much resembled a German scheitholt; it was a square, five stringed type of thing that he said was a church dulcimer. I had never heard that term before. So you have a variety of ideas from people all over the world. It would stand to reason that they brought the characters of the instrument over here with them. I would say the dulcimer was used in Appalachia, the Carolinas, Kentucky, Tennessee, and West Virginia. It was mostly used for entertainment."

Ryan Swisher and Tom Dailey examine a dulcimer.

DESIGN

"There is no standard design, whatever the individual craftsman comes up with. It will affect the sound somewhat. For example, if you have a long narrow instrument, it will have a higher pitched sound. An instrument with a large woody body will have a lot of depth to it. The thicker it is, the deeper the sound. You have more volume with a larger instrument. As far as the number of strings are concerned, it really doesn't matter.

"You will see dulcimers with three strings; and as I've heard from talking to different people, the three stringed dulcimer came into being at the turn of the century. There were only a few craftsmen in the country, and all they made were three stringed dulcimers. I have heard of dulcimers with anywhere from two to eight strings. The most strings that I have used were five.

"There are several things that you can do with the extra strings. You can double over the first string for stressing the melody. On the instrument they are spread 8/16 of an inch apart; if you double over the first string, then you have the first two strings 1/16 of an inch apart. Then when you play, you have these first two strings tuned to the same pitch. This gives you more volume so the melody would carry over the drone strings. The drone strings are much heavier, thus making it hard to hear the melody. The spacing of the string has no effect on the sound at all. It's just on the ease of playing the instrument.

"On a four stringed dulcimer, generally, the first two strings are the you have one melody string and two drone strings on a three stringed dulcimer."

WOOD

"My favorite wood is chestnut, but since it's hard to come by, I usually can't use it. To find chestnut in the condition to use it for an instrument is a rare occasion. It has one bad characteristic in that it splits rather easily. Unless you use it properly, it can cause problems. I found that out the hard way.

"Walnut seems to be everybody's favorite. It has a beautiful color, and it works probably the easiest of any I've used. It takes about any finish. I try not to buy any wood at all. My uncle has a sawmill. I go out, find a tree, cut it down, bring it in, and he will saw it for me. I then have to let it dry for a while. I have some lumber that has been drying for years now.

"Of all the wood I've used, with some exception of hickory, cherry is the most contrary, stubborn wood. It checks out easy. One area will come out smooth, another part rough. Personally, I think I like the looks of cherry better than walnut. It's a lighter wood so you don't lose the detail of the grain, as you do with the walnut. Of course, we talked about chestnut. It works well, has a beautiful grain to it. The one bad thing about it is that it splits. Any of your fruitwoods are good, if you can find a straight and long enough piece to work with. Sassafras is a beautiful wood. I've used it; it looks like oak only it has a purple cast to it. Plum has about the same hardness as oak and most of the characteristics except the color. Sumac, if you can find it big enough, is a pretty wood. It is a lot like walnut only it has a keep purple color. In the middle it has a very pithy core, and you have to work around that.

"Poplar is one of my favorite woods for the top of the instrument. You can use two woods for one instrument, but it is not necessary. Most people make the bottom and sides out of something and the top out of some softwood. Poplar is a nice softwood. It mellows the sound of the instrument, and it is a pretty wood. Poplar has the characteristic in that when it is cut and aged for a real longtime, it turns a deep green color. It works well; I don't think it has any faults, except that it might be a little soft. If you put a hard finish on it though, it soaks into the wood; then it is okay.

"Maple is a lot like cherry in the way it works. You have seen curly maple with the irregular grain. It looks like two grains at once. It is a lighter wood than cherry. It has about the same characteristics; it is contrary, but is makes a beautiful dulcimer. It sort of has a ripple to it. That is what they call windblown wood, or curly maple. It has a really beautiful color."

CONSTRUCTION

"The first thing in the construction would be to gather the material. I get most of my material by just scrounging around. For the wood, I try to find an old building and get the boards or find a good tree and cut it. It is really nice if you can find a real old building because it has better wood. If I cut the tree, I take it to the mill and get it cut; then I let it dry for two years.

"After the material is ready, then I plane the boards to 1/8 inch in thickness to use for the top, bottom, and sides. The bridge, head piece, and tail are cut from the same width stock. The thickness, usually from 1 inch to 1-1/8 inches thick, is determined generally by the number of strings that the instrument will have. Next, cut out, shape, and drill the tail stock, and set it aside. Do likewise with the head stock.

"Cut the bridge to the desired length, or slightly longer. Hollow the bridge out so that the sides are 1 thick and the top is 3/16 of an inch thick. This will allow the frets to seat properly. Sand the bridge, oil it, and attach the frets. The bridge is now complete, except for attaching it to the instrument.

"Clamp the top and bottom section of the dulcimer together to cut the shape. This will keep the dimensions uniform. Glue the bottom and the top of the instrument to the head and tail stock. Clamp on a flat, smooth surface to keep it level. After the glue sets, you are ready to put the buttressing strips on the top and the bottom of the instrument. These should be set in 1/8 inch to allow for the thickness of the sides. These serve as the support for holding the sides, bottom, and top together. Cut and trim the sides to the exact width that the inside height of the instrument is. Steam and bend these pieces to the proper contours of the instrument. The sides are now ready to be glued to the instrument.

"Starting at the tail stock, glue and clamp the sides to the instrument working your way towards the opposite end or the head piece. After the sides are set, unclamp the instrument, and sand the body of the entire instrument, except the instrument, and sand the body of the entire instrument, except forthe bridge.

"Either carve or turn on a lathe the tuning pegs for the instrument. Finish these in oil. The entire instrument is complete now, except for putting the desired finish on and adding the strings."

FINISH

"Types of finish are as wide and varied as the craftsman that makes the instruments. They range from old gunstock recipes, to hand-rubbed oil finishes, to beeswax, furniture lacquers, and the newer polyurethane finishes that are among the easiest to use.

"The finish that I use is a mixture of five parts turpentine, three parts linseed oil, and two parts beeswax. I usually rub three to four coats in by hand, allowing each one to cure before applying the next coat."

ATTACHING STRINGS

"The final step to completing the instrument is to attach the strings. Cut the heads off of small finishing nails. Drive as many nails as there are strings into the head of the stock at a slight angle away from the direction that the strings would come from. Drill a very small hole in each tuning peg. Attach the loop in the string to the nail, stretch across the bridge of the instrument, insert into the hole in the tuning peg and tighten. Do this to all strings.

"The first string (fretting string) is a .008 banjo string. The drones, or the second and third strings, are .013 banjo strings."

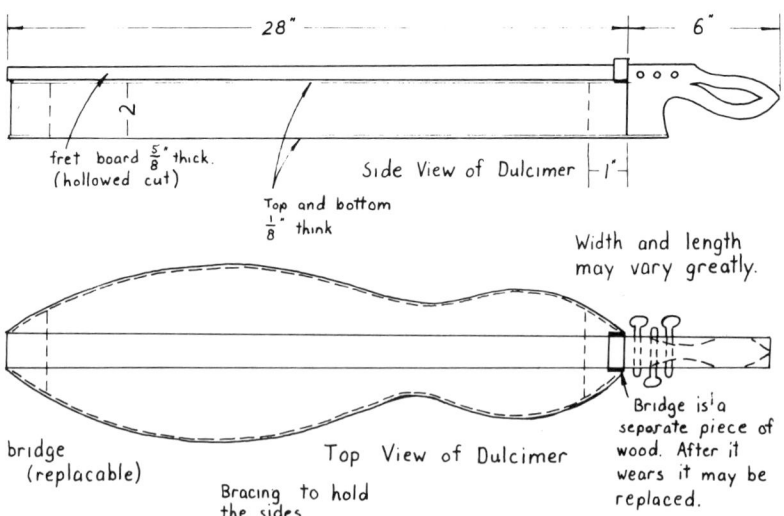

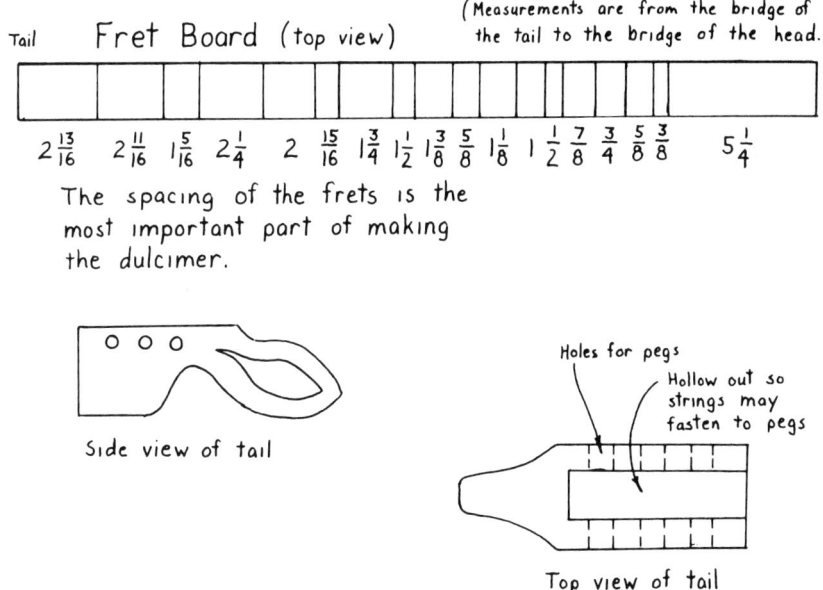

HAMMERED DULCIMER

"The frame of the hammered dulcimer is made from 1/2, 5/8, or 3/4 inch hardwood. The top is made from ½ inch plywood or any close-grained solid wood. Some dulcimer makers prefer a ¼ inch top. This will give a sharper tone.

"The strings can be anywhere from three to six in a group. Number nine piano wire is a good wire to use for the strings. Number seven or eight wire may be used in shorter sets. The end bridges should be at 60 degree angles to the strings.

"The dimensions may be varied to suit the builder. The sound holes are optional."

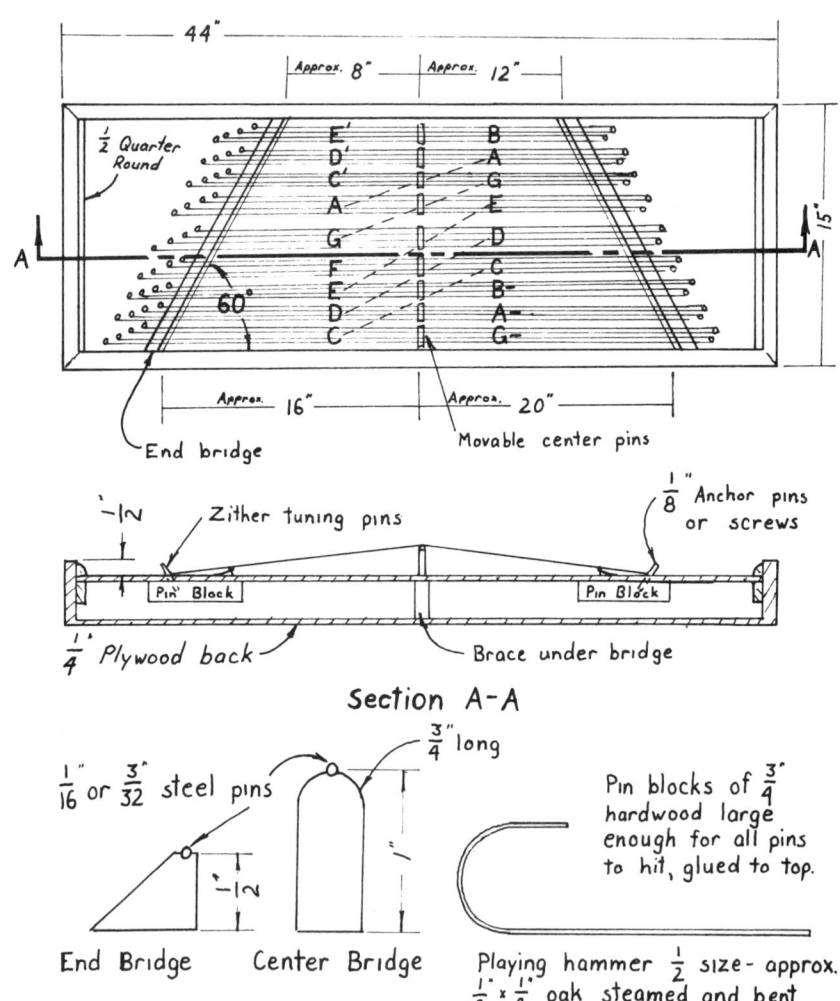

Book II

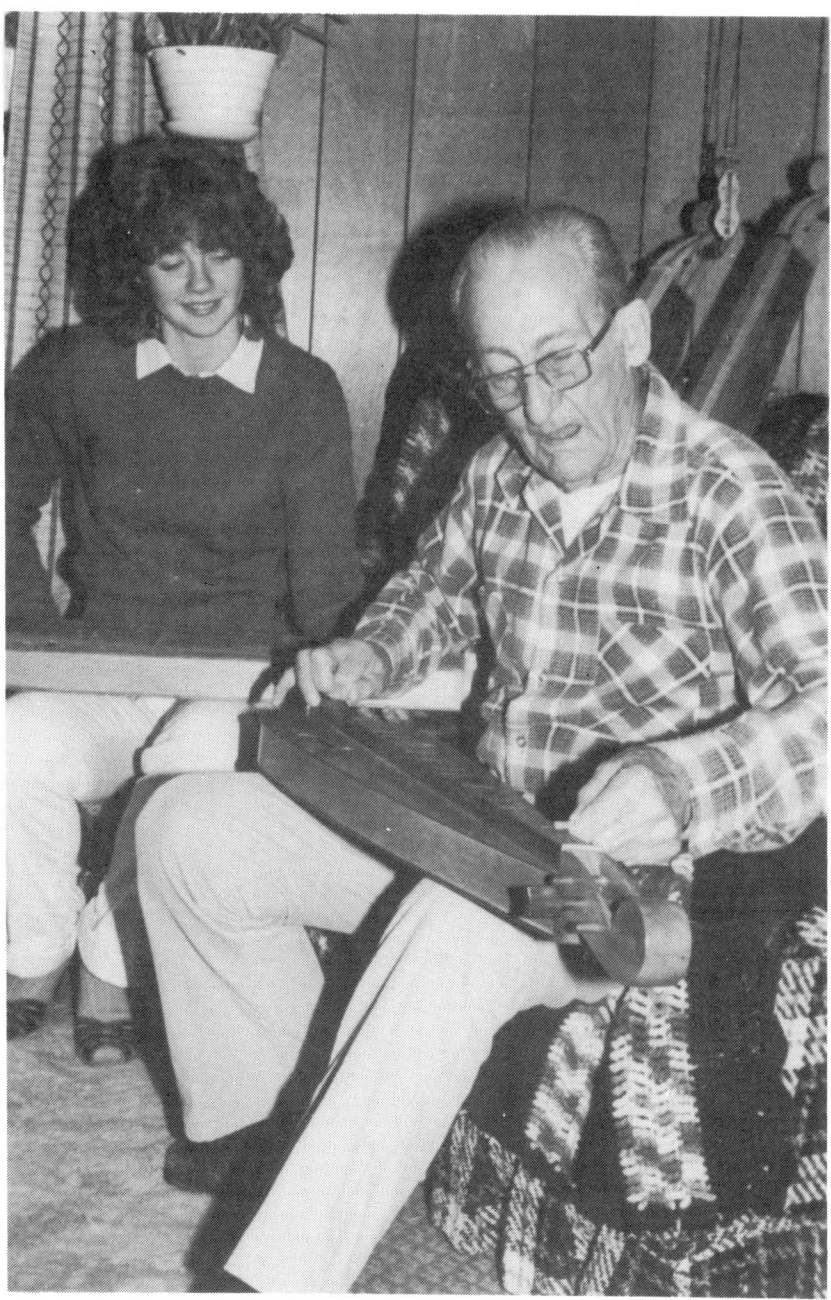

Kelly Riel watches her grandfather Alvin Moore, play one of his dulcimers.

PLAYING HAMMERED DULCIMER

"To play the following songs, strike the string each time the letter appears:"

"SKIP TO MY LOU"
E – E – CC – EE – G
D – D – BB – DD – F
E – E – C – C – EE – G
D – F – E – D – C – C

"RED RIVER VALLEY"
G – C – E – E – G – E – D – E – D – C
C – C – E – C – E – F – F – E – D
G – G – E – E – D – C – D – E – G – F
C – A – B – C – D – D – E – D – C

"OLD TIME RELIGION"
G – A – C – C – C – A – G
C – C – D – D – E – D – C
C – D – E – E – C – D – C
C – A – G – G – A – C – C

Bill Reed, Wood-Carver
by Brian Clegg and Eric Ruf

Bill Reed is a West Virginia wood-carver, whose popular rocking horses have fascinated people with their life-like qualities. He started making crafts when he, along with his brothers and sisters, would sit around the kitchen table and make flowers and owls out of crepe paper. Bill remembers:

"Then the next day, my older brothers and sisters would go out and sell them door to door. I guess in a craft line you can always find something you can do to make a living.

"Some people ask if carving was handed down to me. I answer no, but when I was five or six years old, it was right in the worst part of the depression, about 1930. I more or less started carving then when I was little, with boats and bows and things like that. Just about everything we had when we were children, we made ourselves.

"When I started carving the hobbyhorses, I thought I would come up with something new. You want something that will sell, or hopefully sell. My son-in-law and I battered back and forth and come up with the idea of rocking horses.

"Instead of using plywood and cutting out a rocking horse, I used the concept that might have been developed or used years ago. A man clearing his fields, cutting timber, and he comes home one evening and his wife says we have to have something for our children to play with. So, he hauls in a log and hews out a body, and it ends up as a rocking

Bill Reed carving.

horse. It might have started with a plain block head; I think it is a classic in its own, like a Model T Ford. I made those for about a year; they proved successful.

"I talked to a lady at Harpers Ferry who was 80 years old. She said, that when she was little she had a rocking horse with a plain block head. I would like to think my original ones was very similar to what was used by our forefathers.

"Then after a year or so, I started to thinking. I am supposed to be a wood-carver, and here I am making plain block heads. So, I came up with some hand-carved heads to fit the bodies: a horse, a giraffe, a cow, a dog, and a billy goat. Then I ended up making a nanny goat because of the horns. You have to think of the children getting hurt."

KINDS OF WOOD

"I make the rocking horses out of different kinds of wood. I make them in walnut, oak, cherry, poplar, and pine. The walnut and the cherry are the hardwoods. Poplar is semi-hard wood; but it is still soft, and it will dent up more so than walnut, cherry, or oak. Basswood is the softest; it doesn't have near the grain that some woods have. You can do a lot more detailed work on it. I have more orders for walnut and cherry than any other type of wood.

"To make a horse, if I take a log for the body, I have to split it out with wedges and a maul. Then I would trim it up with a draw knife and use a hatchet to cut out the saddle or seat. I do use some power equipment to cut the legs and rockers. When I first started out, I used to do all that by hand with a hatchet and drawknife. But, in order to increase my productions, I started using a band saw for cutting out the rockers. It also gave me a better ride on the horse; it wasn't such a bumpy ride.

"For carving the heads, I use chisels that I have used for years and years. I use different size gouges, anything from a 3/8 inch gouge to a two, or two and a quarter inch one. I rough them out with a deep gouge, and then I use a lesser size gouge to take the ridges off. Mainly on the rocking horses, I just use gouges and the mallet. On many other carvings, I use a whittling knife, especially for things I can hold in my hand.

"When you carve, you try to work the whole thing. In working with the hobbyhorses, sometimes I'll do a head entirely; other times, I'll do the body and leave the head until last. But, you should work the whole

Bill Reed with one of his donkey rocking horses.

figure all the way around, from head to toe. That way you keep everything in proportion.

"It takes about three days to complete one of the horses, if you count the time to go after the wood, cutting it out, and putting it together. I buy the wood rough sawed and green from a small sawmill. Then I set it aside to dry. I like to use the legs and the rockers just a little bit on the green side and my dowels dry. That way, as it shrinks, it will shrink tight around the dowel. The dowels actually do the holding, but I use a cutting type nail also. I also use Elmer's glue because it sets up pretty fast. Most of them are kept inside, so I don't have to contend with the weather. The glue is just to hold them while I put the dowel in to keep them from starting to work."

FINISH

"I use a commercial finish. I've tried a little bit of everything, but I have had more success with a "finish feeder." A lot of antique dealers use it after they strip a piece of furniture. It consists of a linseed oil, beeswax, and a little bit of turpentine to keep the beeswax dissolved. I think they get the name "finish feeder" because the oil soaks into the wood; it feeds the wood. Then it leaves a surface film of beeswax and that protects the finish. To keep the finish, every three or four months as you see the finish dulling down, you just give it another coat of this "finish feeder." If you use a paste wax, it will build up in the hollows, and they will turn white; this will detract from the finish.

SIZE

The small hobbyhorses stand about 32 inches tall to the top of the head and 20 inches to the top of the body. The length of a small horse is about 32 inches long. The large hobbyhorse stands 42 inches tall to the top of the head and 32 inches to the top of the body. The length of the large horse is about 42 to 44 inches long. The dimensions are pretty close within an inch or two. Not all of them are exactly alike. I try to keep them uniform, so if someone saw a picture of them or would like to order one, they would know basically what they were getting."

EXHIBITIONS

"The hobbyhorses have been exhibited at the Smithsonian, at a

Nanny goat and donkey rocking horse.

gallery exhibit in New York City sponsored by Union Carbide, a promotion in Washington, D.C., and all over the state of West Virginia. I have also attended national and international fairs with them, and I have attended the American and European Craftsman show. They have been sold in almost every state from California to the east coast and from New Orleans to Chicago, and almost all in between. I sell them in about twenty-two shops in the United States. One fellow in California serves as a middle-man and handles the whole west coast for me. The biggest thrill I have had was when a woman come over from Germany and bought one of mine to take back.

This is proof that you can make a living from arts and crafts. It is not a high living, but you can make a living from crafts. It might encourage young people to try a hand at a craft, to know that it is possible that they could at some time make a living from it. I think most kids today are trying to make a million. That is almost impossible unless you have money to start with. But, you can make a living from something like this, if you are willing to work."

Appalachian Recipes
by Karen Easton

PICKLED EGGS

1 cup beet juice
½ teaspoon salt
¼ teaspoon mace
6 hard cooked eggs

1 cup vinegar
½ teaspoon cloves
¼ teaspoon allspice

Place all ingredients, save the eggs, in a saucepan and bring to a boil.

Meanwhile, place the eggs in a quart jar. Pour boiling mixture over eggs. Put on tight lid and cool to room temperature. Place in refrigerator 2-3 days.

LEMON WATER

3 cups boiling water
Juice of 5 large lemons
6 cups ice water
¼ teaspoon vanilla

2½ cups sugar
1 lemon rind, grated
½ teaspoon rose water (optional)
1 cup egg whites

Mix boiling water and sugar in large pan; set over high-heat and boil uncovered, without stirring, 10 minutes. Meanwhile, combine lemon juice, lemon rind, ice water, rose water, and vanilla in a very large, heatproof mixing bowl. When the sugar syrup has boiled 10 minutes, stir into the lemon juice mixture. Beat egg whites into soft peaks. Then beat into lemon mixture. It will be impossible to incorporate them completely because the egg whites are so much lighter than the lemon mixture.

HOOTSLA — EGG SKILLET BREAD

2/3 cup butter
4 large eggs
1/2 teaspoon salt

10 slices bread cut into 1/2 inch cubes
3/4 cup milk
1 1/2 ⁸ teaspoon pepper

Melt the butter in a large skillet over moderate heat, but don't let it brown. Add bread cubes. Turn heat up slightly, tossing gently with a spoon. Fry about 5-8 minutes until delicately browned. Quickly beat the eggs with the milk, salt, and pepper until frothy. Pour into a skillet, tilting it so that the eggs run underneath the bread cubes and to the edges of the skillet. Without stirring, reduce heat and cook eggs 5-8 minutes until lightly browned on the bottom and softly set on top.

WILTED DANDELIONS AND WILD ONIONS (GREENS)

4 tablespoons bacon drippings
6 wild onions
1/4 teaspoon salt

3 quarts dandelion leaves
1/4 cup cider vinegar
1/8 teaspoon pepper

Melt bacon drippings in large heavy kettle over moderate heat; add dandelions 2-3 minutes until lightly glazed. Add vinegar, salt and pepper. Toss to mix, cover, and simmer over low heat 10-15 minutes, or until dandelions are tender.

WAFFLES

2 cups flour
1 teaspoon salt
3 eggs separated

4 teaspoons baking powder
1 2/3 cups milk
6 tablespoons melted butter

Beat yolks well and add milk. Add all dry ingredients. Add melted butter. Fold in stiffly beaten egg whites. Bake in hot waffle iron.

FUNNEL CAKES

2 cups milk
3 eggs
3½ cups flour
pinch nutmeg
½ teaspoon salt
2 teaspoons baking powder (optional)
2 tablespoons sugar

Beat eggs and milk. Add remaining ingredients and mix. Drop in the shape of a coil, through a well-greased tin funnel into hot oil and fry. Brown on both sides. Roll in cinnamon and sugar.

BRICK OVEN GINGERBREAD

¾ cup butter
¼ cup molasses
2 cups flour
1 teaspoon ginger
½ teaspoon salt
1 cup sugar
1 egg
2 teaspoons baking soda
1 teaspoon cinnamon

Cream together the butter, sugar, and molasses; beat in egg. Sift flour with soda, spices and salt, and stir into the creamed mixture. Chill dough until firm enough to shape. Pinch off bits of dough and roll into small balls the size of walnuts. Roll balls in granulated sugar. Place 2 inches apart on greased baking sheets or on hot oven bricks. Bake 12-15 minutes at 350 degrees.

ROASTED CHESTNUTS

To roast a chestnut, first puncture it with a knife or sharp object. Otherwise, it will explode in the fire. Cover the chestnuts with coals from the fireplace and leave them about five minutes. Peel shell off and eat.

BOILED CHESTNUTS

Peel the shells off the chestnuts. Put the peeled chestnuts in peanut oil for about five minutes at 350 degrees. Drain and salt before eating.

MOLASSES POPCORN BALLS

Put three tablespoons of butter with two cups of molasses and ⅔ cup of corn syrup into a saucepan.

Boil the mixture (280 degrees) until a little syrup dropped into cold water forms a brittle mass.

Quickly stir the mixture into the popped corn (most people pour it over the corn.)

Form the popcorn into balls. Let balls set until firm.

MOLASSES TAFFY

2 cups of molasses	1/8 teaspoon of soda
1 cup sugar	4 tablespoons butter
¾ cup of water	½ teaspoon vanilla

Cook the molasses, sugar and water slowly to the hard ball stage (260 degrees). Stir during the latter part of the cooking to prevent burning.

Remove from fire. Add butter, soda, and vanilla and stir to mix. Then pour it onto a greased pan.

When the taffy starts to cool lift it up from the pan and fold (edges) towards center. Lightly butter fingers before working with it.

When it is cool enough to handle, pull until it becomes light in color. The pulling will take 15-20 minutes. The more you pull, the better.

Stretch the taffy into a long rope and cut it with scissors into small pieces.

Candle-making
by Fred Mayer

The first candles were nothing more than fat with possibly a wick made of plant fiber or animal fiber, like wool or even human hair, which would be used for the wick. Later, candles were dipped in beef tallow. The colonials would collect beef tallow after butchering in the fall so they could start dipping candles. They would save every little bit of fat they could. Then it would be put in a big crock or a big kettle or something similar. Then when it was time to dip, they would move everything outside. The women usually dipped candles. If there were any small children who were too young to go out and hunt or too young to handle an ax, they would help dip candles. Candledipping is not all fun because when you're doing it with beef tallow or any kind of animal fat, the smell is rancid. The strong odor is added to the fumes and the smoke coming from the fire. The smoke changes directions as the wind blows and chases you around the kettle.

The first step in candlemaking was preparing the wick. The wick was usually cotton, it was woven very, very tightly. Sometimes it would be a long spun thread.

Several different apparatus were used to dip the candles. However, the most common one was nothing more than a piece of wood or a branch; this was about two feet long. This would have two or three wicks hung over it. Then you placed two long poles between two chairs or something to make a drying rack. This left the sticks hanging over these with the wicks on them. The candlemaker started with the

Fred Means dipping candles.

front row of wicks and dipped it in the tallow. It was taken fast because if left too long, nothing accumulated on the wick. It melted off in the pot. The first one was dipped and hung, and then the next one down the line. After all were finished the candlemaker went to the first one. It would be cool enough to dip again.

When these candles were burned, the tallow had a strong odor. They also smoked a lot and burned fast. Later on, it was discovered that putting beeswax in them would take away some of the smell. They also burn more evenly and longer so it was half beef tallow and half beeswax.

The process of dipping didn't really change at all till later on in the mid-eighteenth century; then the use of molds made of pewter or tin began. The inside of the mold would be greased and the wick placed in it before the beef tallow and the beeswax were poured in it. After the candle was poured and cooled it was carefully pulled out of the mold.

When they wanted to make a torch or something like that, many times they would take cattails, the round spiked part, and dip this in the tallow (or the beeswax) and saturate it. One of these would burn for an hour or longer. These would be used in funeral processions and at night for outdoor lighting.

When cotton was not available swamp rushes were sometimes used. The outside was stripped away, leaving a pithy center, about the thickness of a pencil lead. This was dipped and became known as a "rush candle." It burned faster than the cotton.

The candles were usually made in the fall because that was when the butchering was done. When the cooking was done the fat was saved. A good supply of it was necessary because it was used in both soap-making and candle-making.

Harold Reed, Printer

by Lori Hall and Scott Morgan

It was one of those cold February days when we visited Fort New Salem's print shop to talk to Harold Reed, the village printer. Besides being the official printer at the fort, Harold is an art instructor at Salem College.

We found him to be interesting and knowledgeable about the old art of printing.

OLD SALEM

"At one time there were four printers employed to work here at Salem, West Virginia. This area was settled by some Seventh Day Baptist people. We have read that they had a printing shop here in 1792. It would have been a wooden press similar to the one we have here. I am not sure how they supported four printers here. They probably printed for the church and had the early newspaper."

STARTING IN PRINTING

"A friend and I decided we would like to have some type of craft or hobby that was a little different than the ones you see in shows or fairs. So, we decided letterpress printing isn't done anymore; it was such an important part of our colonial heritage, especially in the struggle for independence with Great Britain. Printing on a wooden

Harold Reed demonstrates the American Press.

Book II

The American Press

press played a very important role. For months we sketched, read, and wrote for information concerning early printing. The most we could find were photographs and drawings without dimensions. So, we compared similarities and differences, and finally made our own plans.

"Even the museums that have the old presses don't demonstrate on them. They will usually just have the remains of part of an early print shop.

"Since we are taller than our ancestors, we made our press a little higher. However, the wood in ours is similar to some of the earlier ones.

"Most of the press is wood. The largest pieces are poplar (because of the lighter weight), and the other pieces are oak and pine.

"Leather is used on the press as hinges and also for the belt which moves the bed of the press.

"A metal threaded screw is used. The pitch of the screw must be just right in order to give the type punch an impression on the paper."

PRINTING

"The first step in printing is setting the type. You hold the composing stick like and artist would hold his pallette (at right angle to put individual letters in). When you pick up a piece of type to put it in, it will be backwards. So, you are setting it upside down and backwards. There is a notch in the edge of the type. Most of the notches are large enough to feel. You shouldn't have to look at each letter. You just feel it to know where the notch is to place it in the composing stick.

"Between each line of type you put a thin strip of wood or metal depending on how much space you want between the lines. Once your composing stick is filled with about two or two and a half inches of type, you slide it out onto a metal tray.

"After you fill the tray or galley, then you put a metal frame or chase around the type. Then you finish the filling (the space) around this with pieces of wood, to get it ready to go on the press. So you handle it a lot.

"The chase is moved to the bed of the press, centered, and "makeready" prepared. "Make ready" is a process of trial and error in getting a good impression on the type surface. A print is first made on the frisket. Then that area is cut out, forming a protective stencil which keeps the other prints clean of ink.

A composing stick.

"Before the paper can be printed on, it must be dampened. Every other sheet is dunked in water, and then they are stacked. The paper is then placed in a press to distribute the moisture. If the paper is too wet, it will not leave a good impression. If it is too dry, it can break the type.

"The paper is then placed on the tympan and held by two or more paper tabs which act as guides to keep the paper in place. The type is then inked with ink balls.

"The type case is like a typewriter in that it is not in alphabetical order. When you look at the case, you will see large compartments and small ones. The large compartments are in the center. They are the most frequently used letters. The letters Q, L, and K are over at the side in the small spaces because you don't need them very often.

"If you know the arrangement, you simply pick it out and put it in the composing stick. You shouldn't have to look at the letters. You assume they are in the right box.

"If they are in the wrong box, that was the apprentice's fault. When you put the type back, you cannot throw them. You handle them gently because they can damage easily.

"It is usually called lead type, but it is an alloy. Lead by itself is too soft. If you drop it on the floor, sometimes you can break the edge off.

OLD PRINTING AND LETTERING

"The British learned the printing trade from the Germans. The first type was what we call a "black letter." Today, we might compare it to Old English. It's hard to read, but it resembled the writings and manuscripts. Think of the monks in a monastery doing all their careful lettering. They were using a black lettering, and that is what the early type resembled.

"In 1500, they came along with Roman typeface. Roman type was available from Germany and was used until in the early 1700's.

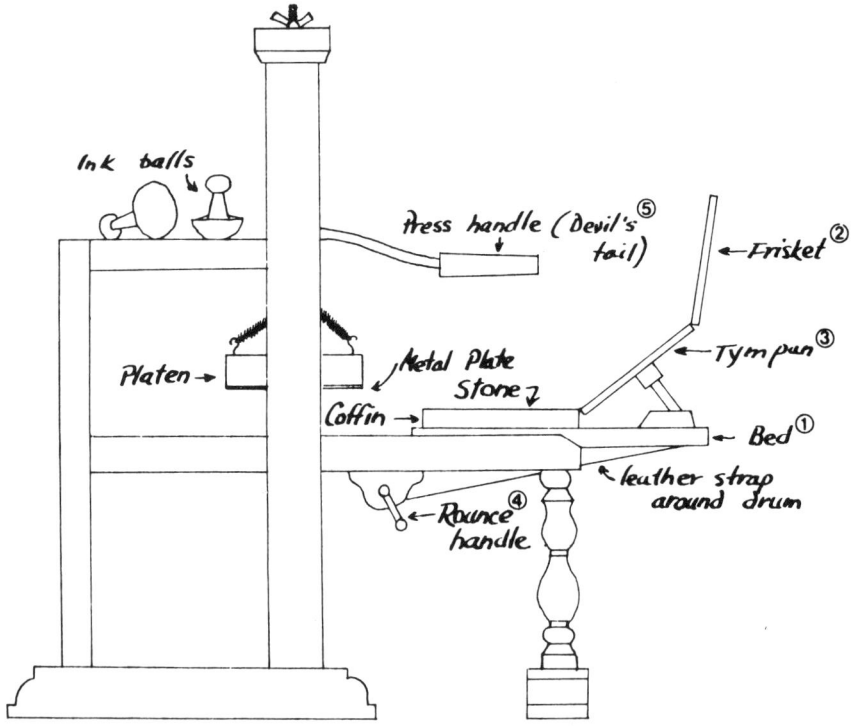

"The frisket is folded down on the tympan, and then onto the bed of the press. The rounce handle is turned, which cranks the bed under the platen. Then the press handle, or devil's tail, is pulled, applying pressure from the platen to the bed, causing the type to make an impression on the paper. The press handle received its name, the Devil's tail, because of its curved tapered shape. The term, "Devil's Helper," is applied to a printer's apprentice, which possible came from the saying, "Angels must write; the Devil must print."

"In the 1700's, Caslon (lettering) type was introduced by William Caslon. He was an engraver in London who decided he would design a new type. He worked on his type for 14 years before he issued a specimen sheet to show the public his work. His work was so much clearer and easier to read than the Dutch or German type that many American printers preferred Caslon type. His type is used today because it is open faced and easy on the eyes. Stevenson-Blake is a British company that still maintains the Caslon foundry.

"We were British long enough here (America) that we still used the long "S" until about 1810 or 1813. If any printer had the long "S," he used it. He didn't throw it away to buy new type. The long "S" is confusing, especially today. Ben Franklin argued to keep it. He thought it gave the page variety.

"About 1835, the long "S" was considered the classic form and it had a brief revival, but it didn't last. You needed to know where it was used and what the rules were to be able to use it. In a small book or newspaper, it is hard to tell if it is a full crossbar or a half crossbar. So, it is difficult to tell if it is a long "S" or a small "f."

"In a twentieth century shop, the arrangement of the capital letters reflects the original Roman alphabet. It would be alphabetical until you get to the **I's** and **J's; I's** and **J's** are interchangeable. There was no U in the original Roman alphabet. They also used a **V** for the letter **U**.

"In some of the early title pages of the books, the printer's name would be John, and it would be spelled J-o-h-n.

"Speed in setting of the type would be very important. If you were working for a newspaper, you should be able to set type and communicate at the same time and not make any mistakes.

OUR *Colonies* are Bleſſed with an abundance of *Willing People;* a Few are willing to *labour* & the Majority are willing to let Them.

"There are over 10,000 typefaces in the United States today. We have a lot of other typefaces (besides Caslon) that will still fit our time period (here at the fort)."

APPRENTICES

"The printers, as well as a lot of the other trades, had apprentices. Many of them were indentured apprentices. That doesn't always mean a slave; they either had their passage paid from another country to work off, or they were indebted in some way.

"The length of the apprenticeship depended on the rate of paying and how long you were going to stay in that shop. Many young people started as young as twelve years old. In order to set the type, they had to stand on a little stool to reach the type case.

"Apprentices in all trades ran away all the time. Many of the older papers give enough description so you can identify them. Usually the amount of money they offered as a reward indicated they didn't really care whether they got them back or not, but they still printed a notice that they were missing.

"They would usually run away because of working conditions. If they started as young as twelve years old, they were usually away from their family or parents. They were just too young to be in that sort of child labor situation."

NEWS

"Before we had a thing such as a post office, you could post a letter with the printer. Activities of a community centered around the printer. New information from another community or town came to the printer's office.

"The print shops had a bulletin board on the front of them. If a printer would print an item for a customer, he would usually post a copy out there also. That was his method of advertising.

"Any public announcement, they called a "broadside." It sounds like a big sheet, but today we would call it a pamphlet or a handbill. Any information for public distribution was a broadside, even the Declaration of Independence. That was done for the public, so it was a broadside. John Dunlap did it in 1776.

"If it were just a few sheets, they would roll them up to carry them.

PUBLICK NOTICE!

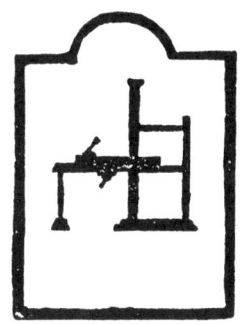

BE it Known that a £5 REWARD ſhall be Paid for the APPREHENSION of a *Runaway Indentured Servant,* a Preſs-Man by Trade. He appears pretty much Pitted with the Small-Pox, wears his own Hair & is much Bloated by Drinking, to which He is moſt uncommonly Addicted; He ſtoops much & has a down Look, is very Talkative when Drunk and remarkably Stupid.

Inquire at the Office of *The American Preſs.*

Samples that we find in museums today still have the evidence of being folded or stored for many years.

"You could have a broadside printed if you got mad at a neighbor, when a new shipment of goods arrived, or your livestock strayed. Anything that you needed to get the word around you'd get a broadside printed.

"If you didn't have enough money to have them distributed, you could post them on the boards. (Boards were bulletin boards at different places in the community where news would be posted.)

"An unusual thing about the early newspapers that we have discovered is a lot of items or articles were several weeks old, but they were new to the area. They usually didn't print much about local happenings. That was gossip, and you were expected to know that.

"During the Revolution most of the information was about battles and raids by the British. News of battles farther north or south were printed. Many small community papers printed the Declaration of Independence in columns as a news item.

A a b c d e f g h i j k l m n o p q
r ſ s t u v w x y z .   a e i o u
A B C D E F G H I J K L M N O
P Q R S T U V W X Y Z .

a e i o u	a e i o u
ab eb ib ob ub	ba be bi bo bu
ac ec ic oc uc	ca ce ci co cu
ad ed id od ud	da de di do du

In the Name of the Father and of the Son, and of the Holy Ghoſt. *Amen.*

OUR Father, which art in Heaven, hallowed be thy Name; thy Kingdom come, thy Will be done on Earth, as it is in Heaven. Give us this Day our daily Bread; and forgive us our Treſpaſſes, as we forgive them that treſpaſs againſt us; And lead us not into Temptation, but deliver us from Evil.   *Amen.*
    1 2 3 4 5 6 7 8 9 0 .

"This sheet printed on the press (at Salem) is a hornbook page. It formed a primer for children in the 1700's. It was mounted on wood and protected with transparent horn, and usually hung at the child's waist."

CHAPBOOKS

"I think that the first prints that really became popular were the cheaply made and crudely illustrated **chapbooks**. Those were stories such as **Robinson Crusoe**. They weren't so strictly religious in their teachings, but became very popular. It was more of a pleasant relaxing reading than the strict church teaching."

HORNBOOKS

"They printed a lesson sheet and put it on a board. Probably in most countries they were known as paddle boards, named after the wooden paddle shape. The British gave it the name **hornbook**. Paper was expensive, and that printed page would become soiled pretty quickly when children carried it.

"By the time it came to this country, we knew it as a hornbook. And even before they were printed, they were written on parchment and paper and then fastened to that little paddle shape. There are records of so many dozens of hornbooks coming on a ship. Then later, they were printed in this country.

"The printers could print several of these on one sheet, if they had the type, and then they cut them apart later.

"You could go to a printer's shop and have a book simply printed. The pages were a loose bundle of a book. Someone else would have the bindery. If it were just a few pages, the printer's children or wife would sometimes stitch them together."

WRITING SUPPLIES

"The printer's shop was usually the place to go to buy writing supplies too.

"Most people had their own geese in their barnyards, so they could produce their own quills. But the printer sold ink and other supplies.

"It is hard to write with a quill since we are used to putting a lot of pressure on pens or pencils today. A quill encourages you to write with a light touch.

"The most common quill is the goose quill. There were more geese around the homestead than turkeys, but a turkey quill worked.

"If you stick the quill into hot sand, it will strengthen it and the tip will last longer. Just leave it in the sand a few minutes.

"There are all kinds of recipes for preparing goose quills. Some of them, you cut the tips off and boil them in water with some alum for up to three hours. The lower part becomes clear and hardens a little. Then you cut the tip and shape it.

"Another recipe says to bake the quill in the oven at pleasure. We don't know how hot or how long, but again, heat strengthens the writing tip so it will last longer.

"Some feathers will have two or three inches of the hollow part of the feather, so you can cut several new tips on one quill.

"Early printers usually marked their work with their own logo, or trademark. This design is the logo of the American Press.

"The early printers used signs or marks on their works. Also, every shop had a trade sign on the outside because a lot of people couldn't read, but they could recognize the sign of the blacksmith, the apothecarian, or the different shops. The sign on the front of one shop has the silhouette of a green tree.

"The printers also used marks to show their work. The marks originally were put in the back of the book, but they became so decorative and elaborate that they moved it to the title page.

"Many of the early marks were based on a cross or an arch. The figure four was also in there somewhere, usually. The symbol was called a 'colopon.'"

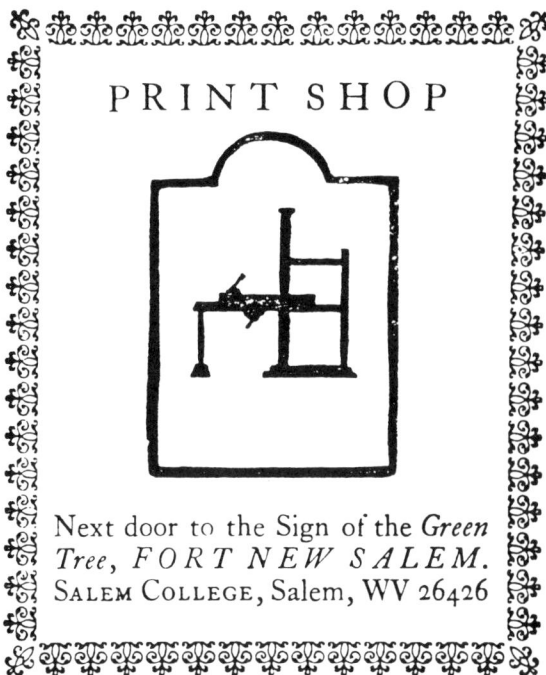

Return address for the official envelope of the print shop at Fort New Salem.

Making An Applehead Doll

by Drema Lemley and Roberta Russell

The art of making dolls is a long-standing tradition with the Duckworth family of Mineral Wells, West Virginia. Mrs. Virginia Duckworth is the fourth generation continuing the craft.

The idea of the applehead doll is over a hundred years old. Johnny Appleseed was thought to have taught Mrs. Duckworth's ancestors, and she has carried the tradition on for 41 years.

It is presumed the craft originated with the Indians. Johnny Appleseed learned the art of making the doll from them and then taught it to other people as he traveled.

Besides being used as toys, the dolls served many purposes. Known first as weather prophet dolls, the pioneers carried them westward. When the weather was going to be wet, the head of the doll would become soft and sticky. The head would become hard and dry during an arid spell. Thus the early settlers could predict the weather.

Also called fashion dolls, the dried applehead doll would be dressed in the latest style and taken west, so the women could copy the clothes.

The dolls were also used to carry seeds. A small packet of seets would easily be lost on the trip west. A young child would latch on to the doll, and when the settler reached his destination, the seeds in the head of the doll would be cut out. The hole would then be plugged with wax or mud. By this means, the apple tree was spread across the United States.

In some parts of the country today, the heads are dipped in shellac or varnish. This method ruins their usefulness as weather prophet dolls. However, the heads of Mrs. Duckworth's dolls are dried naturally and left that way. A child could eat one of her dolls' heads without harm.

DIRECTIONS

The first step in making the doll is carving the apple. Yellow or Red Delicious or Rome Beauty apples are used. The apple must be a firm one, and the stem must be left inside or the apple will rot. After peeling, carve two wedge-shaped slits, about one fourth of an inch apart to form the nose. Then the eyes are hollowed out. An area beneath the nose is hollowed out to form the mouth and chin.

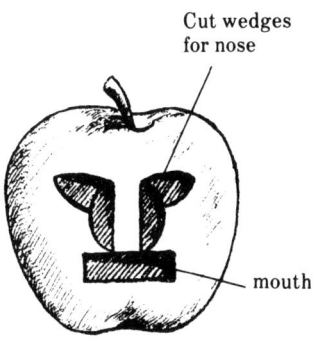

core apple before drying

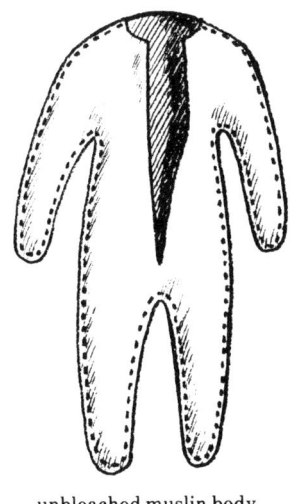

unbleached muslin body

If the apple does not dry to suit, it can be recarved later.

The apples are hung in a dry place for about three months. They deteriorate to approximately two thirds of their original size. No two apples ever dry alike.

Mrs. Duckworth usually does not recarve the apples, unless she is making a character doll such as Martha Washington.

The bodies of the dolls are made from unbleached muslin, cut into a human form. The forms are stitched around the edges and turned inside out with a rug hook.

The skeleton of the doll is made from pipe cleaners so that the finished doll will bend in any direction. The pipe cleaners are rolled in cotton and inserted into the limbs of the sewn form.

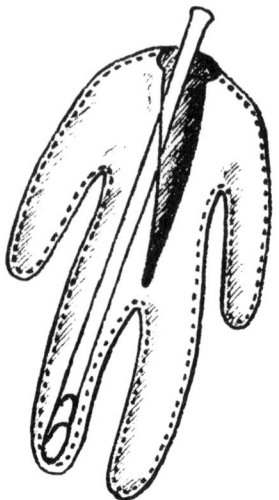

rughook used to pull arms and legs inside out

bend pipe cleaner

roll pipe cleaner in cotton or quilt batting

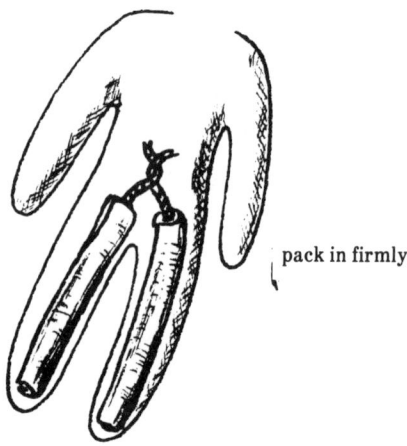

pack in firmly

The arms and legs of the doll are joined to a pipe cleaner backbone, and the empty spaces are filled with cotton.

Fill in with cotton

tightly here

loosely here

Since the dolls are bendable, the stitching on the back must be reinforced. This is done by tying every third stitch.

tie every third stitch

A nail covered with glue is then inserted in the neck, sharp end up. A dowel stick may be used for this purpose if the doll is for a child.

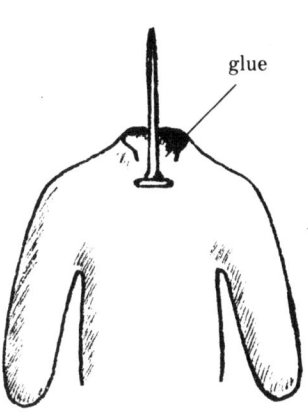

dowel stick or small nail

glue

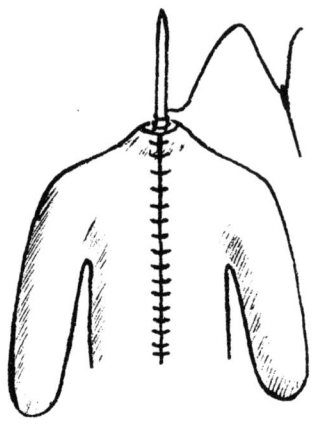

wrap thread

The two edges of the muslin form are wrapped in thread.

After the body of the doll has been stuffed and sewn up, the next step is dressing the doll. The female dolls wear pantaloons and slips. The pantaloons are stuffed to shape the body and sewn to the doll around the waist.

baste around waist to body

pad pantaloons

slip

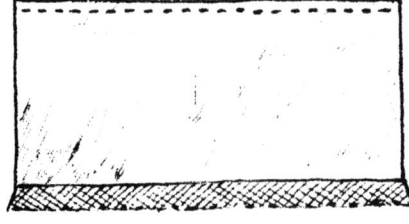

baste and pull, leaving most of the gathers in back

15" x 5¾"

The slip is made from a rectangle of cloth 15 inches by 5¾ inches, hemmed with lace on one side.

The other side is basted, then gathered at the waist of the doll. Most of the gathers are put in the back.

For the colonial doll which requires a wasp, or slender, waist, the doll is made narrower by winding elastic or thread around the body.

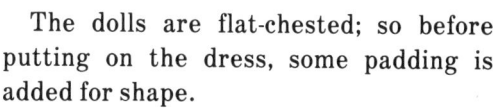

baste to body of doll

extra padding for women

The dolls are flat-chested; so before putting on the dress, some padding is added for shape.

The dresses are pulled on from the bottom, and more padding is added before the garment is sewn closed.

pad with cotton for backs of shoulders — sew up with very small stitches

The dolls may be dressed in a variety of ways. The most frequently used styles are colonials, pioneers, farmers, mountaineers, and character dolls.

Mrs. Duckworth has a basic pattern she used for the women's dresses, but she is constantly designing new ones for special dolls. The fabrics she most frequently uses are gingham, calico, and denim.

Since all of the apples dry differently, it is necessary to find a head that suits the body. The heads are finished by adding hair and eyes. Holes are punched with sharp instruments. Cloves, the heads of which have been broken off, are then inserted for the eyes.

The mouth and nostrils are carved into the head with a pin or small knife.

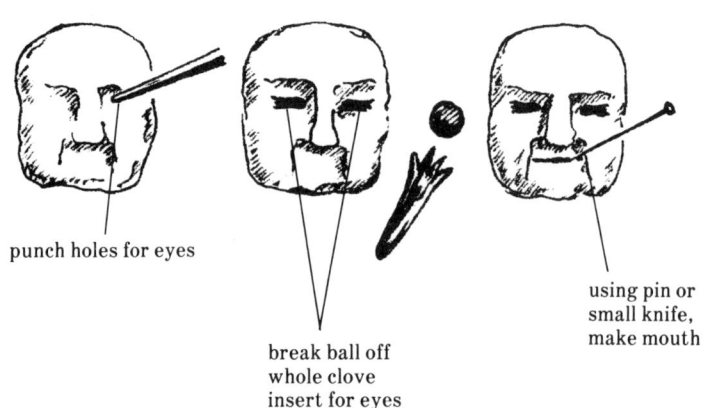

punch holes for eyes

break ball off whole clove insert for eyes

using pin or small knife, make mouth

The hair of the dolls is made from small mohair wigs. Cotton may also be used for this purpose. The hair is gathered into a bun at the back of the head and is held in place with a small pin.

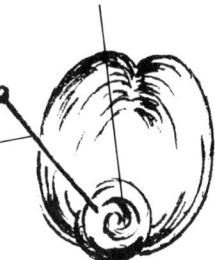

wrap ends around finger to form bun

pin until glue dries

find a head that suits body

apply glue to nail, then stick on head

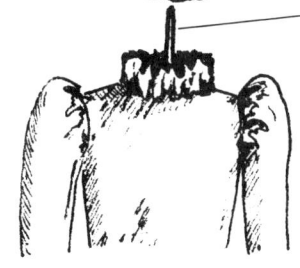

Glue is applied to the nail protruding from the body, and the head is pressed down onto the nail.

Most of the old-fashioned dolls wear bonnets. The bonnets are made with a circular stitched brim or a slatted brim, with small cardboard slats which hold it stiff.

make stitches on sides of bonnet

black felt
fold here

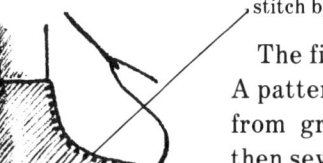

stitch by hand to body

The final step is adding the doll's shoes. A pattern is cut (as shown in the diagram) from gray or black felt. The shoes are then sewn onto the feet.

George Pinkham, Wood Craftsman
by Steve Lockhart

In the rustic setting of his workshop, we met with Mr. George Pinkham. It was a cool afternoon, and George was ready to start his demonstration. He was the epitome of the pioneer spirit: brown bristly beard, blue jeans, flannel shirt, and red suspenders.

George Pinkham taught us much, not only about rustic craftsmanship, but more importantly, about the pioneer's spirit, and his fight for survival. He spoke of the traditions of wheel and buggy-making and the unforgettable time he spent with the Amish.

"Probably the most prominent wood craftsmen in this area were the farmers. They might have had a little woodshop in a shed or a barn. (Many even brought sleds, etc., into the house in the winter months to repair or rebuild). There were a few cabinet-makers in Clarksburg, but most of the people (in this area) made their own things.

"When the Europeans came, they hadn't had access to the vast amount of timer they had here. The huge quantities of timber are mentioned in journals. In a journal of one of the first settlers, it is mentioned that he came across a tree that had fallen across the path and he couldn't see over it while on horseback. So, you can imagine how huge that tree was if he couldn't see over it while he was on horseback.

"Now, they had a vast amount of timber. They needed to clear the

George Pinkham splitting a log.

timber, and the American blacksmith invented the poleax. It was one of America's first inventions.

"If you ever come across an ax that looks like a tomahawk and looks hand-forged, it is probably a very primitive piece.

"The woods were a threat to the colonials. The crops couldn't grow for them. It was a place where predator animals could hide. So they wanted the land cleared. The Scotch-Irish settled this area, and they just stripped everything."

HEWING A LOG

"To hew a log, place two small logs under each end of the log that is being hewn. Then drive a hewing dog into each end of the log to be hewn and in the smaller logs. These (hewing dogs) will hold the log from rolling around as you work on it.

"After the log has been secured, you mark it with chalk lines the size you want the finished log. Then you score the log with an ax every six inches. You stand on top of the log while you score it.

"After the log has been scored, you take a broadax and cut out the sections between the scores.

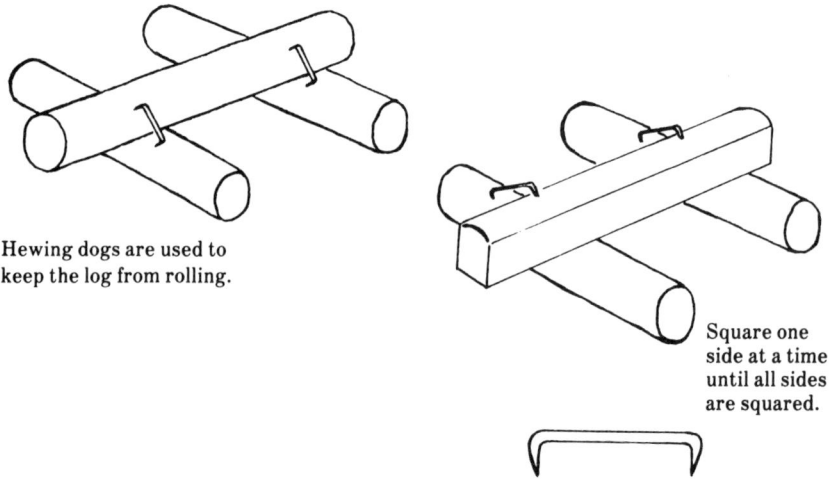

Hewing dogs are used to keep the log from rolling.

Square one side at a time until all sides are squared.

Hewing Dog

"The broadax handle is bent to keep from skinning your knuckles up as you hew the log.

"Of course, you are working with a green log. All of the chips come right off. If you didn't score the log, it would be like cutting a whole slab off at a time.

"A good logger, who is good with an ax, will have the log square and true when he is finished. You shouldn't be able to see the score marks. The fewer score marks you see, the better the fellow was that was hewing the logs.

"If you want a finer job than you can get with a broadax, then you use a "foot adz" to finish the log."

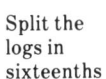
Split the logs in sixteenths

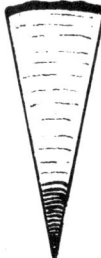
Cut the heartwood off. Then split the bolt in half. Keep splitting the bolt till you get the desired thickness of your shingle.

SHINGLES

"Most of the shingles we have come in contact with are made out of white oak or chestnut oak.

"To split the shingle you cut your logs into what we call 'bolts.' You divide your log into sixteenths, about like you do a pie. Then you cut the heartwood out. Then you are left with what you call a bolt. Then you put your fro in the middle of these bolts and rive your shingles out.

"The wood needs to be clear for your shingles with no hidden twists or knots in it. Sometimes, it you have a hidden knot inside, then you can put it in a shaving horse and use a drawknife and shave that knot out. By doing this, you make it really smooth.

"The smooth side would go down on the bottom side of your roof. You want the rough side up because of the grooves in the wood. The grooves act as little gutters and the rain runs right off.

"To put the shingles on, you lay a row of shingles across the building and then go back and lay another row on top of them to cover the cracks. So, for every row of shingles there is actually two rows.

"A lot of old folks will tell you that if you had a real cold day and it was snowing, the snow would blow under the shingles or you could look up and see the stars through the roof. Once it rains, the moisture in the air would draw the shingles back down.

"You lay your shingles when there is a new moon and the roof won't leak."

BUILDING A LOG HOUSE

"When someone got ready to build a log cabin, several men would go out and cut the trees. One man would pick out the trees he wanted for certain uses. Then, they would haul them onto the site.

"Then, the next day they would have four men doing nothing but notching. They would each have a corner. Then, they would have the roof on by evening. The second day, they would do the inside carpentry work and maybe even do a fireplace. By the third day, they would be finished."

HICKORY SPLIT BROOM

"To make the hickory split broom take a piece of pignut hickory and peel the growth layers back with a penknife. Determine the length you want the bristles and peel it back that far. After you have enough bristles, then cut the center core out.

"Then go above the bristles and peel more in the opposite direction.

These will be bent over the first ones to make a better finished jog. Make a band from the inner bark to hold the bristles in shape.

"To finish the broom take a draw knife and work the handle down to the desired size."

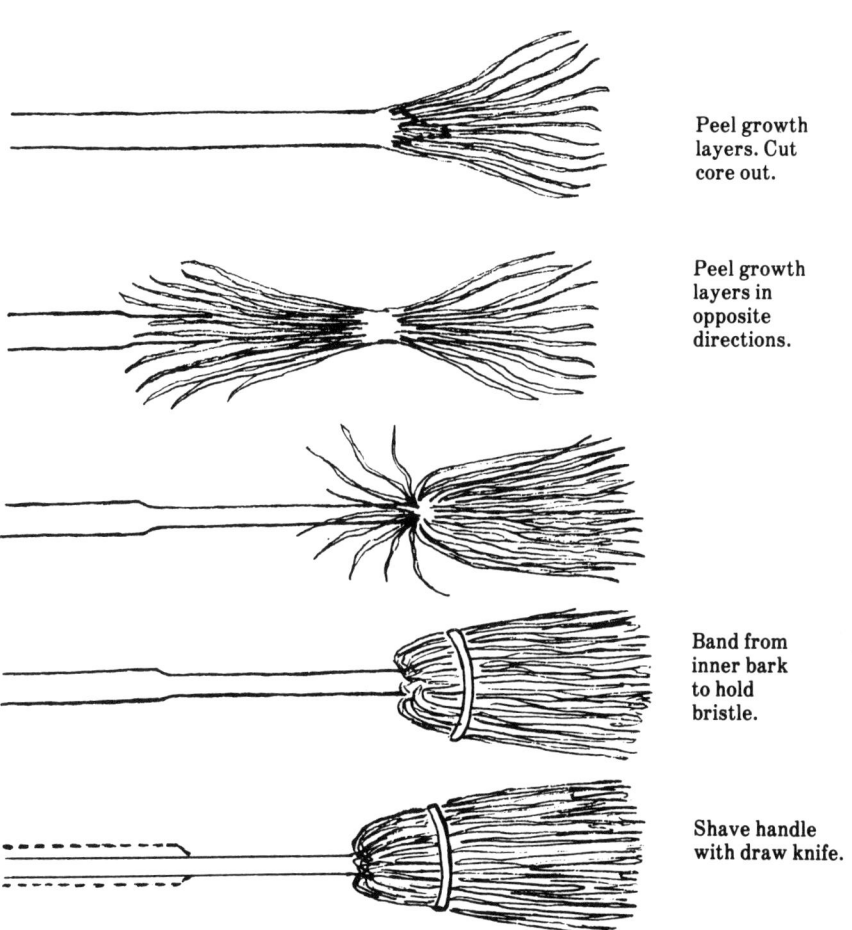

Peel growth layers. Cut core out.

Peel growth layers in opposite directions.

Band from inner bark to hold bristle.

Shave handle with draw knife.

BUGGY WHEELS

"I had the opportunity to go to Pennsylvania and learn to make buggy wheels from the Amish.

"We purchase all our hubs and spokes. The traditional hub had a metal casing with wood inside. So, the boxing on your axle had to be greased constantly. The hubs they use now have bearings inside and are much easier to take care of. There is not so much deterioration from the inside. The bearings only need to be greased every one or two years.

"The spokes are egg-shaped; they do not lay flat, but slightly curve up. This causes what we call a "dish." The dish puts the hub farther inside than what the rim of the wheel is (concave form).

"Traditionally from the Civil War period, they used a rivet to hold the spokes together. Now they use bolts. Bolts make it easier to tear the wheel down to make repairs to it. It also makes the construction of it much easier.

"Some hind wheels on a buggy are forty-two inches, and the front wheels are thirty-eight inches. There is always a four inch difference in the front and back wheel of a buggy.

"Most of the tools I use to make the buggy wheel were developed around the 1870's."

DIRECTIONS FOR MAKING A BUGGY WHEEL

Step I. To begin making the buggy wheel, you need a stand to the hub of the wheel to.

Step II. The spokes which go in the wheel are egg-shaped, rather than being oval. With the end grain of the spoke being egg-shaped, this helps form the dish of the wheel. You and tenon the spokes into the hub so they fan out around the hub, and you secure the spokes to the hub with bolts every two spokes.

Step III.   If you are making a 42 inch wheel, you cut the spokes so the height of the wheel is 42 inches.

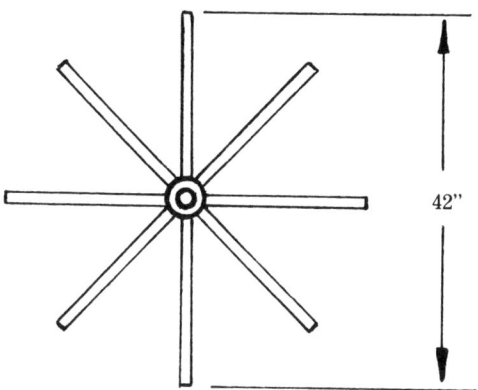

Step IV.   After the spokes are placed in the hub, you put a cone-shaped instrument on the brace and bit and sharpen the ends of the spokes down (like a pencil sharpener). This gives the hollow auger a place to start.

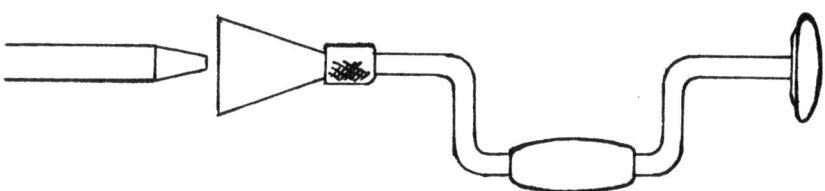

Step V.   After the spokes have been sharpened, then put the hollow auger on your brace and cut the spoke in 1¼ inches or the width of your fellows.

Step VI. Next your fellows are steamed and bent into a 42 inch circle.

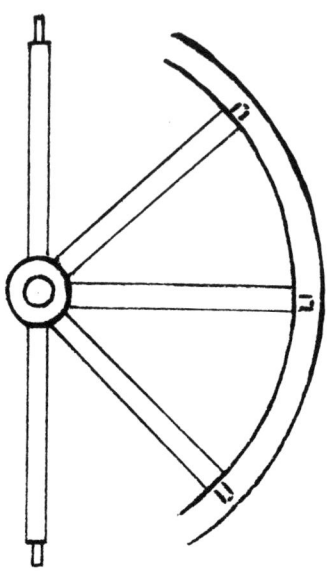

Step VII. Mark the fellows where the spoke will hit it, and drill the holes in it (fellow) for the end of the spokes to go into.

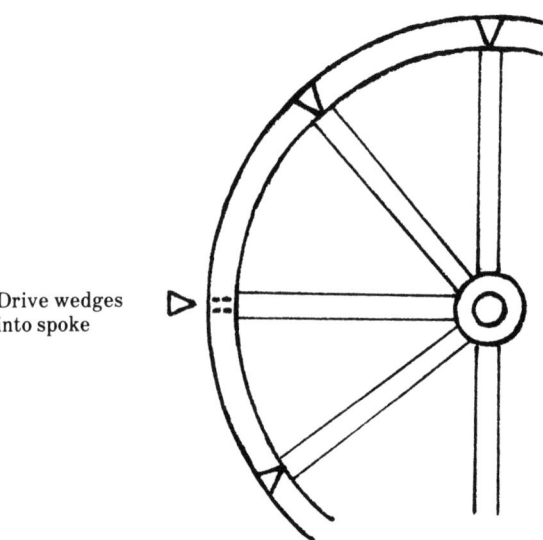

Drive wedges into spoke

| Step VIII. | Put the fellows onto the spokes, and then drive small wedges into the spokes to hold it secure. |
| Step IX. | Take a traveler and measure the outside diameter of the wheel or fellow. |

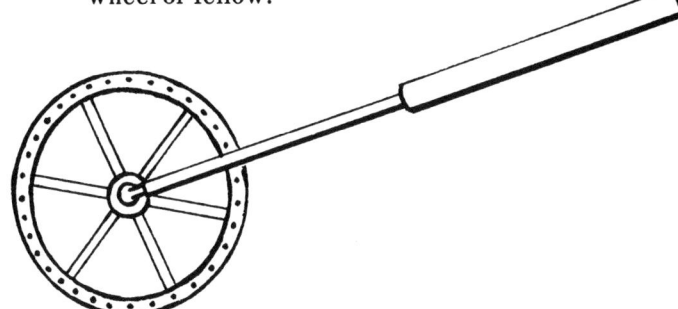

Step X.	After you measure the wheel with the traveler, add 1/16 of an inch to the measurement and mark the tire-iron off with this measurement (with 1/16 inch added).
Step XI.	Cut the tire-iron at this measurement.
Step XII.	Roll the tire-iron in the tire-iron machine to get the proper curve to it.
Step XIII.	Weld the tire-iron together.
Step XIV.	Heat the tire-iron to a black hot.
Step XV.	Pound the tire-iron onto the fellow while it is still hot.
Step XVI.	After the tire-iron is pounded on, then cool it immediately with water.
Step XVII.	As the metal shrinks, it will also create the dish-shape in the wheel.
Step XVIII.	Bolt the tire to the fellows.
Step XIX.	Where the fellows join together, put a fellow plate on to hold them.

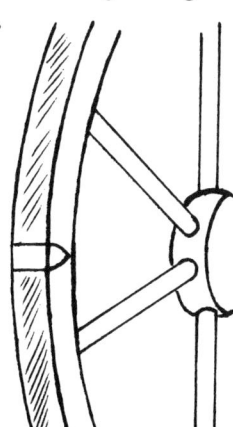

Making A Corncob Doll
by Paula Star Key and Tina Lowers

While looking for examples of traditional American heritage dolls, we discovered the corncob dolls created by Mrs. Joyce Wines. Directions for making the dolls are included in the following story.

"The American heritage dolls included corncob, sock, dried apple,

Eric Ruf, Steve Lockhart and Joyce Wines.

cornhusk, clothespin, and other wooden dolls. I have experimented and come up with my own ideas. I don't know if there is any particular history. To make the doll, the pioneer used the complete corncob without cutting it. The cob was kept intact. For the face, they used a piece of coal to blacken in the eyes, popcorn for the nose, and fixed the mouth with some other color. It wore old-fashioned bonnets and long dresses.

"My version is just a little bit newer. I cut the corncob into sections and drill a hole through the cob to attach the arms. the original dolls just had sleeves and didn't have arms made into it like the ones I make now.

"To make the doll, I first cut the corncob into sections. The body is from four to five inches long. Then slice another cob into sections of about one half inch pieces. These pieces will stand on the end of the corncob and be glued into place for the face.

Lady corncob doll.

"After selecting and cutting the corncob into pieces, put it into a pan and bake it in the oven for an hour at 250 to 350 degrees.

"After baking the cobs, use a stiff toothbrush and brush the dry husk off. It is dry and will come off easily. The cobs are baked to kill bacteria, molds, or insects that get on the corncobs.

"Some people use knives to cut the cobs, but a saw will work better. After the cobs are baked, they become very hard, like wood.

"The eyes are made of little northern beans or are painted in. The beans also should be baked at 100 degrees. If you bake them too high or too long, they turn brown. Sometimes, they will burst in the middle."

1. For the eyes use a marking pencil or acrylic paints. If the face gets wet with the marking pencils, it will bleed into the corncob.

paint eyes and mouth

small bean

girl's head

paint eyes and mouth

small bean

man's head

2. For the men corncob dolls, use fake fur and comb it in for the hair and the beard.

Book II 129

3. Use Elmer's glue to attach the head to the cob. Glue it in place; several hours later, glue the sides again. Fill it in around the sides. It's very sturdy because the corncob is porous.

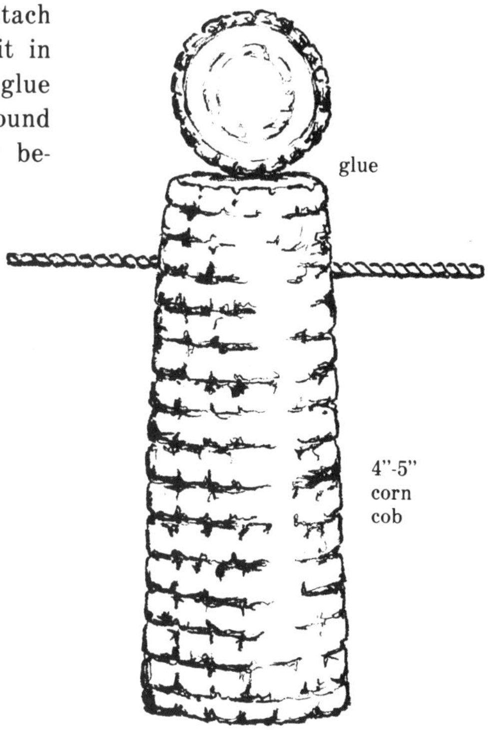

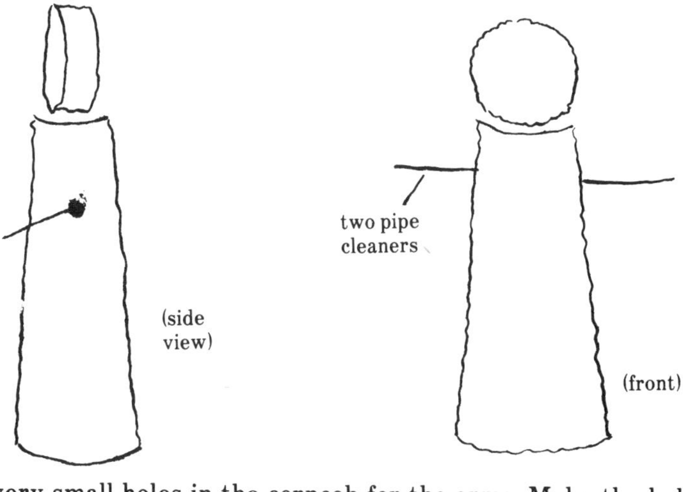

glue

head — small cross-section of corn cob

(front view)

4"-5" corn cob

drill hole for pipe cleaners

(side view)

two pipe cleaners

(front)

4. Drill very small holes in the corncob for the arms. Make the holes only large enough for two pipe cleaners to go through. Use a very small drill bit so that the two pipe cleaners will just barely go through. Do not use the big decorator pipe cleaners; use actual pipe cleaners.

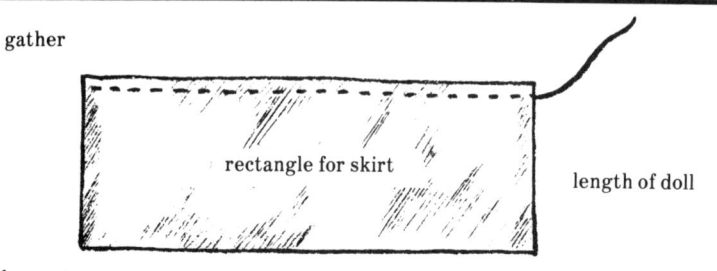

5. To make the slip, gather the material at the top and place it on the body. Then draw the string tight, fixing the gathers until they're even. Take the thread around the body and tack it in the back.

Put slip around doll. Wrap thread tightly several times around body and arms.

Loosely draw the thread around the body and around the arms. This will secure it. Then you can design any type of dress you like.

On the blouse, first hem the sleeves; then sew up the sides of the sleeves and the sides of the dress, or the blouse of the dress. When that's done, gather the skirt, attach it to the blouse, and sew it up the back. Then, hem it according to the length of the doll.

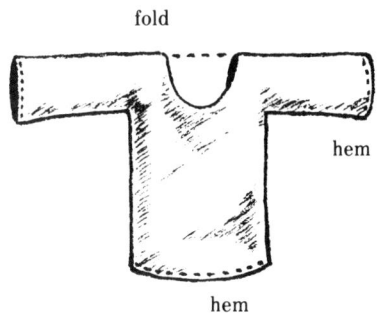

(shirt)

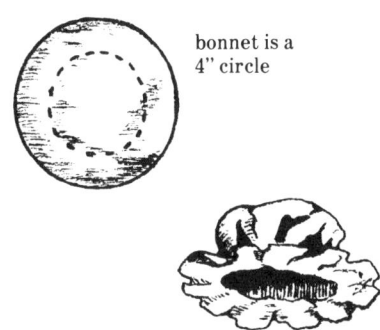

bonnet is a 4" circle

A four inch circle is used for the bonnet. Sew lace around the edge, then gather to fit the head; then place it on the doll's head and glue it into place. Put glue around the edge of the bonnet and attach a half inch of lace.

gather out edge and glue to girl doll's head

Decorate the front of the dress with a piece of lace. Get a double-edged lace for the front of the dress so there are no raw edges. For the bonnet, use single-edged lace or a hemming lace.

I had to come up with a new hat for the man. Everyone kept calling him a scarecrow because of the high pointed hat; that was the old hillbilly hat.

circle of material

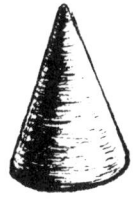
cone of material (brim)

The hat is just a felt circle. Then, make a cone out of hand-stitched felt. The cone is glued to the top of the circle. To make the old-fashioned hat, take the point and push it back down through the hat.

Man's hat is cone glued to circular brim.

complete hat

Man corncob doll

For the man corncob doll, use fake fur for the beard and wrap material around the corncob for the trousers. Use rope for the belt. There's also a handkerchief in his pocket.

Use all cotton material, if it's at all possible. Many different styles of dolls can be made from the one basic pattern.

folklore

Home Remedies
by Roberta Russell

Our medicine cabinets are full of patented and prescription drugs that are far from what our ancestors had to rely on for good health. In his best seller, *Folk Medicine*, D.C. Jarvis says:

> "Our pioneer ancestors discovered the rudiments of their folk medicine in the healing plants sought out by animals suffering from alimentary disturbances, fever, and wounds."

Thus, the "home remedy" developed because of a need for medication when the doctor was not just a call away. A reliance on nature for a cure, without chemicals, was necessary. Many of the following remedies have been used not only by those who contributed them, but also by their parents and grandparents before them.

HEADACHE

Hiding a dishcloth under a rock cures a headache.
Tie something tight around your head for a headache.

EARACHE

For an earache, squeeze the juice from one white onion. Warm the juice in a teaspoon (not too hot). Pour the warm juice into the affected ear. The pain will soon be gone.
Blowing warm smoke into the ear from a pipe or cigar will ease an earache.
A warm salt bag eases an earache.

WARTS

Rub a piece of dishcloth on a wart and buy the cloth. When the cloth rots, the wart will disappear.
To remove a wart, cover it completely with fresh milkweed juice. It works best if the wart is bleeding slightly.

SINUS

1 Tablespoon of brown sugar
1 Teaspoon of salt
1 Pint of boiled water
Put in an atomizer and spray in nostrils or use as nose drops.

COLD

Drink snakeroot tea to break up a cold.
Boneset tea will doctor a cold.
Wear an asafetida bag to ward off colds.
For an infant's cold, roast an onion in a wet cloth on hot ashes until soft; peel the outside off, and mash it. Apply on a cloth to the hollow of the child's foot.
Lamp oil, pure hog lard, turpentine, and camphor mixed together and greased on the chest makes a good remedy for a cold. The mixture should be covered with rags and should be kept hot in some way. In the days before the heating pad, stacks of maga-

zines were heated on the stove and used as a source of heat. This helped cure pneumonia also.

COUGHS

Wild cherry bark was boiled to make cough syrup.
One with a cough should wear flannel next to the skin.
A cough syrup may be made from any combination of vinegar, honey, licorice, horehound candy, and rock candy.
For a cough, take half a pint of warm milk fresh from the cow. Mix in a fresh egg, a little sugar, and nutmeg. Drink it warm first thing in the morning.
For whooping cough, take equal parts of honey, sweet oil, and vinegar. Simmer together over the fire a few minutes; then bottle for use. Dose—a teaspoonful as often as necessary to allay coughing.

CONGESTION

For chest congestion, apply a paste of mustard and flour to a cloth to cover the lungs. Remove when skin is pink.
Apply clean horseradish leaves on chest. Cover with hot pancakes and then a dry towel. Remove when skin is pink.
Sniff warm salt water to relieve nasal congestion.

SORE THROAT

Kerosene and lard will ease a sore throat, but do not wrap it or the skin will blister.
Gargle with warm salt water to ease sore throat.
For hoarseness, take four ounces of grated fresh horseradish, saturate it in a pint of good vinegar overnight; then add half a pint of honey. Bring it to the boiling point; then strain and squeeze out. Dose—one or two teaspoonfuls several times a day. This treatment if very good for hoarseness, loss of voice, and all ordinary coughs.

FEVER

To induce sweating and reduce fever, make tea of herbs (mullein, boneset, or yarrow).

ACHES AND PAINS

Wear or carry a buckeye to keep away rheumatism, or cure it.

To ease arthritis, drink crushed pokeberries and whiskey.

Apply vinegar to ease the pain of sunburn.

Ague Cure (chills) - One pound each of sassafras, sarsaparilla, spikenard, and wild cherry bark. One half pound of bloodroot. One fourth of an ounce of mandrake. Four gallons of water. Boil all down to one gallon, strain, and add one quart of rye whiskey and one half of an ounce of oil of peppermint. Adult dose — one tablespoon three times a day.

ARTHRITIS

1 Cup of honey
1 Cup of vinegar
(Mix together)

Use four teaspoons in one cup of warm water and drink in the morning for arthritis. Honey made from the goldenrod flower is the best.

CUTS AND BURNS

To stop bleeding, bind on goose feathers, pressing them into wound. Allow them to remain until they come off.

Placing a spider web on wounds will stop bleeding at once.

Tie up fresh cuts with warm ashes from the stove.

Clean a fresh cut with pure turpentine to keep it from getting sore.

To stop a burn, scrape a potato on the area—the potato will become red.

Take fresh lard, any quantity, and work it into a quantity of powdered soot—about a tablespoon of soot to an ounce of lard—and apply. This is one of the best applications for burns and scalds that can be made.

Apply chewed tobacco to a cut to stop the bleeding.

Chew slippery elm bark until it becomes slimy; place it on the cut.

SORES

Mix fat meat and turpentine to put on a sore to draw infection.

The membrane from the inside of an eggshell is placed on a boil to draw it to a head.

To stop a bruise, scrape a potato on the injured area—the potato will become black, and the skin will not bruise.

An ulcer-like sore that spreads, usually in the mouth, can be healed quickly by applying peroxide.

To heal corns, apply rattlesnade or mud turtle oil.

TEETH

Dip a toothpick in oil of clove and chew with the sore teeth to ease the pain.

For a toothache, burn a piece of paper on a plate. Using a piece of cotton, wipe up the sweat from the plate and put it on the tooth.

INFECTIONS

When a contact's brother had a sand briar lodged in his foot, the briar worked its way from the sole up through the top of the foot. To clear the infection, his mother placed cow manure on top of the sore.

Pine pitch is good to draw out infections.

Mud placed upon a wound and allowed to dry is good for drawing out infections. This remedy was used on animals. Horses with cuts on their legs were often led through deep mud.

For deep cuts or severely infected wounds, the best method for drawing infection was to bind fat meat to it. In some instances, a freshly killed animal was used. The cut was cleaned and filled with medicinal herbs. Then a small animal (a rooster, for example) was split and bound to the cut so that the insides of the animal were against the wound. This compound was sometimes left for several weeks.

Another "dead animal" cure is the cure for a snakebite. When bitten, catch and kill the snake. Split the snake, and tie it over the bite to draw the poison out.

OTHERS

To stop nosebleed, put a cold key on the back of the neck.

Mudpack will ease a bee sting.

Kerosene on your wrist and ankles will keep the chiggers off when berry picking.

Relieve the pressure of blood under a bruised fingernail by piercing the fingernail with a red-hot nail or needle.

When ill, a pleasant tea can be made from dried wintergreen leaves, peppermint leaves, spearmint leaves, or pennyroyal leaves.

A cure for ringworm—yellow dock root or leaves steeped in vinegar will cure the worst case.

A muskrat skin worn over the lungs, with the fur side next to the body, is a relief for asthma.

Drink sassafras tea in the springtime to thin the blood. Your blood is thick in the winter, so it must be thinned.

Tie a bag of asafetida around your neck to prevent diseases.

A poultice for pneumonia is made from polecat grease and put on the chest. The polecat is killed, skinned, and cooked to render the grease.

STERLIZATION OF BANDAGES

Sterlization of bandages has always been a problem. The usual method was to boil them in water. Mrs. Laura Russell told us of an unusual method of sterilization used by her grandmother, Mrs. Jerome Dean, of Leachtown, West Virginia. Her idea was that dry heat was better than boiling. She placed her bandages in an oven and heated them. Then she sealed the sterile bandages into jars, just as if they were canned foods.

Old Wives Tales

The old wives' tales, or superstitions, constitute the best forms of folklore.

These ideas are basically inspired by a fear of the unknown. To explain a mysterious or startling occurrence, our ancestors came up with tales involving beliefs in magic, chance, and fate, Many of these beliefs have survived generations in spite of scientific arguments against them.

BAD LUCK

Each stitch you sew on Sunday, you will have to pick (remove) with your nose when you die.

Three on a match brings bad luck.

When a girl marries: If you change the name and not the first letter, you marry for worse and not for better.

A whistling girl and a crowing hen are sure to come to no good end.

Don't allow a cat in the house with a sleeping baby. It will draw the baby's breath away.

To carry hoes, axes, or shovels in the house is bad luck.

To open an umbrella in the house is bad luck.

When you move to another house, don't move the broom. It is bad luck to move the broom.

If you spill salt, throw some over your left shoulder to prevent bad luck.

A child born on the thirteenth of the month was supposed to die or bring disgrace.

The burning of sassafras wood in the fireplace will bring destruction upon the family by fire or flood.

GOOD LUCK

A cricket in the house brings good luck.
To find a four-leaf clover is good luck.
A picked-up pin will give you good luck.
Carry a four-leaf clover or a buckeye for good luck.
Put a horseshoe over your door to let luck come in. Do not hang it upside down or your luck will go out.

WEATHER

Red sky at night — sailor's delight. (good weather)
Red sky at morning — sailors take warning. (stormy weather)
If hornets' nests are built near the ground, the winter will not have much snow.

If the water from a flood falls very rapidly, two more floods will follow.

If flood waters recede leaving ice on the banks of the river, another flood will follow soon to pick up the ice.

When a groundhog sees his shadow February 2, there will be six more weeks of bad weather.

Planting by the signs will yield a better crop.

Summer lightning from a southerly direction means 'hot weather.' lightning, no rain.

If it rains on Monday, it will rain at least four days of the week.
A tough apple skin means there will be a hard winter.
Bees stay close to their hives when it is going to rain.

If there is a circle around the moon, it is going to storm. If there is one star within the circle, it will be twelve hours before the storm; if there are two stars within the circle, it will be twenty-four hours till the storm.

If the moon is on its back, the weather will be dry.

When the snow adheres to the bark of a tree, it will remain on the ground as many days as the number of hours which it stays on the trees.

If frogs are heard before March 19, St. Joseph's Day, expect six additional weeks of inclement weather before constant good spring weather appears.

Showers before seven in the morning clear up before eleven.

Mackerel sky — not long dry. (Mackerel sky — tiny white clouds, high and close together)

WISHES

Make a wish on a turned-up hem and on the first star at night.
Wish on a new moon, and your wish will come true.

FRIENDSHIP

Knives as gifts must be accompanied by a coin (penny) to keep friendship from being broken. If you give a gift with a sharp point or cutting edge, it will hurt your friendship, so always "sell" it for a penny.

Dropped silverware means you will have a visitor: teaspoon, a girl; tablespoon, a woman; fork, a boy; and a knife, a man.

Never let a pole come between friends.

DEATH

Deaths come in three's.

If a dog howls outside a window, there will be a death in the family soon.

When the master of a house dies, someone should tell the bees in their hives that the master is dead, or the bees will leave.

If a person is dying, he must not lie on a feather bed.

The last person to leave the cemetery will be the next to be buried there.

Superstitions

Some people have a special talent to "buy" your wart for a penny and remove it.

If you don't handle toads, you won't get warts.

If you thank a person for the gift of a living plant, the plant will die.

If you are outside the house in the evening, come in before the dew falls. Night air is unhealthy.

Don't start anything that cannot be finished by Friday.

For good luck, eat new cabbage cooked with a dime on New Year's Day.

To make a cat stay in a new home, butter its paws.

Eating burned toast will give you curly hair.

Put a fresh horse hair into the watering trough outside the barn, and it will turn into a snake.

Every white spot on your fingernails is a lie you have told.

When walking, if you step on a crack, you will break your mother's back.

March borrows three days from February to finish killing the old cow.

If one plays with fire in the evening, he is sure to wet the bed that night.

Recipe for happy babies: "Plenty of sleep, plenty of milk, and plenty of flannel."

If a child talks to itself, it will be healthy.

The sex of your baby can be determined as to whether you carry it "high" or "low" in the abdomen. Girls are generally carried high in the abdomen; boys are carried low.

Home remedies and wives' tales are more common than one might realize. At one time, they were known by all who lived in the southern hills of the Appalachian region.

In reading this type of folklore, one must remember that this is an oral tradition. It is told, not read, by people who have passed it down to us. No printed word can give originality or fascination to a folk remedy or superstition.

recollections

Spring Harvest Dinner, With Edelene Wood
by Lori Harpold

"Springtime belongs to the Appalachian wild foods cook just as certainly as fall seems a time for Indians to gather their wild provender for the long winter ahead.

"Chickweed is good raw or cooked until about the first of April. I have particularly enjoyed gathering chickweed at that time for a wild food seminar that I helped to establish in northern North Carolina. When gathering this plant, I always ask my friends to cut it off with a knife or scissors. This makes clean greens to use instead of having to labor cutting off the roots in the kitchen. Also, although most farmers would love to get rid of it, cutting off the top does no damage.

"Winter-cress is also called water-cress. In North Carolina, this plant with the Latin name **Barbarea vulgaris** is known as "Creasy greens." It is also available during the winter, but most Appalachian greens gatherers think of it as being at its best in March, and at most early in April, before it starts to bloom. I have a secret of my own in connection with winter-cress. I like winter-cress crowns. While digging winter-cress, most Appalachian cooks dig up the whole plant, which at the edible stage is a rosette of leaves. When I make a mistake and dig up the whole plant, I trim the root and the leaves, ending up with the crown from which the leaves emerge. I wash these and because everything seems to be extremely tender at this time, I sauté the crowns in butter, salt to taste, and serve as a vegetable.

"I have tried winter-cress in many ways using the crowns, along with the leaves, for interesting hors d'oeuvres. For leaf hors d'oeuvres, spread thin cream cheese on crackers and lay a tiny winter-cress leaf on top for decoration.

"Young dandelion crowns may be used in the same way as winter-cress crowns; the tiny leaves may be used along with crackers and cream cheese for the leaf hors d'oeuvres.

A dandelion salad recipe from Zoar Village, dating back to 1817, stated that one needed a large wooden bowl of fresh dandelion greens; 4 slices of thick bacon, diced; ¼ cup country butter; ½ cup thick cream; 2 hen's eggs, beaten (or 1 wild turkey egg); small handful of salt (heaping teaspoonful); dash of black pepper; ¼ teaspoon paprika; 1 teaspoon brown sugar (more if coarse, unrefined); and ¼ cup apple cider vinegar.

Carefully wash dandelion greens. Use only the tender new growth. Shake dry and place in wooden bowl. Pan fry bacon; crumble into small pieces, and place over greens. Warm butter and cream in same skillet (after pouring off the grease), using low heat. Add remaining ingredients to cream mixture. Increase heat and cook until mixture thickens, stirring constantly. Pour hot dressing over the greens. Toss and serve a real "back to nature" salad.

"I have served hundreds of wild foods dinners, and this particular technique of fixing dandelion greens is not only an art but, varied according to the cook, the most acceptable.

"I have made dandelion root coffee and used the winter roots for vegetables. I have made hundreds of dishes with the new leaves, buds, and flowers; one recipe for dandelion muffins was developed by my mother, Hazel Wood, whom I was always able to persuade to try some new wild food idea. She incorporated one cupful of dandelion blossoms in a regular muffin mix. The blossoms must be pulled from the green crown before being used.

"Advice for poke salad from the Commissioner of the Georgia Department of Agriculature was to peel the young poke salad shoots when they were about six inches high. Wash the shoots and leaves, put in a pot, cover with water, bring to a boil, and drain thoroughly. Add fresh water, bring to a boil, add salt to taste, and lower the heat. Cover pot and simmer vegetables for about five minutes. Season with butter; add more salt and pepper, if needed.

"Other wild greens that can be enjoyed in early spring include milkweed leaves and later, buds of the flowers. Both can be parboiled, then cooked with a little salt and butter. I have eaten dock greens, chickory greens, violets, lamb's quarters, elderberry, blackberry, and nettles. Each of these greens has a host of followers. Many other people favor mixtures of greens, again treated as one does dandelion greens, Zoar Village style.

"What is parboiling? The old Appalachian cooks sometimes called this pareboiling. Whatever one calls it, it means boiling in water; and in the case of the greens, one throws off the water three times or more until the greens are tender.

"Remember what every good wild food cook knows: NEVER EAT A WILD PLANT UNTIL YOU KNOW IT SO WELL YOU WILL NEVER MAKE A MISTAKE AS TO ITS IDENTITY."

Wild Food Recipes

VIOLET BLOSSOM PUNCH

Gather several quarts of violet blossom heads (no stems) and place in quart jars. Cover with boiling water. Add lids, and place jars in refrigerator. Twelve hours later, strain out blossoms. Make a syrup of remaining "extract" by combining ½ lemon and 2 cups of sugar for each cup of extract. Bring to a boil and bottle in sterilized jars. Now, for the punch: Combine one quart of this violet syrup with one large bottle of carbonated cola and an equal amount of cold water. Add lemon juice to taste (one small bottle lemon juice) and lots of ice.

HOT MOUNTAIN TEA (WINTERGREEN)

Gather one quart of wintergreen leaves. Red leaves are all right, even preferable, if you want a color to your tea. Add boiling water to the quart of leaves. Let set two days. You will notice a slight fermentation taking place. Heat tea and leaves in jar, placing jar in another container of hot water. When hot, sweeten, and serve. It will have a pink color if you use only red leaves.

VENISON IN PASTRY

The original venison roast at my first meal was an uncomplicated roast made by my mother the day before the dinner and sliced ready to serve. Later, she made a version of Venison Wellington which should be remembered. Here is what she did:

Mix together 2 lbs. flour, 2 sticks butter, 12 tablespoons shortening, 1⅔ tablespoons salt, and 4 egg yolks with enough water to make a light pastry. Let set in refrigerator for 3 hours. Then roll pastry into a sheet. Add following meat mixture plus 1 lb. fresh mushrooms. Roll, seal, and glaze with egg white just before baking at 425 degrees for 10 minutes, 350 degrees for 10 minutes, then 325 degrees for 45 minutes. Drain and serve cold. Filling: 5 lbs. ground venison, 4 eggs, 1⅔ tablespoons salt, 2 cloves of garlic, 1 teaspoon thyme, ¼ teaspoon ground bay leaf, ¼ teaspoon allspice, 3 tablespoons peppergrass seeds (green), 1 cup cognac, and 1 cup minced onions. Beat this mixture until completely mixed, adding cognac last. Let rest while pastry is being made. (This is venison deluxe and is a dish deserving special applause.)

WHOLE BAKED BASS

We used a three pound bass for our first wild dinner and prepared it this way: clean and prepare for cooking but do not cut into pieces. Coat outside and inside of fish with melted butter. Sprinkle with salt and pepper. Place fish on a large piece of foil. Sprinkle with lemon juice and wrap fish in the foil so juice will not escape. Bake at 400 degrees for 45 minutes or until well done.

MILKWEED GREENS OR GREEN BUDS

Pinch off tender young leaves for milkweed greens, making sure that you are getting the leaves of common milkweed, not one of the other types of milkweed. Or, if the new green buds are setting on, pinch these off and use instead of greens. Treat both the same for a beautiful dish of greens. I once had a friend who referred to the cooked buds as "river broccoli." Parboil milkweed by pouring boiling water on them and pouring it off three times. Then cook buds in small amount of boiling water to which you have added salt and butter. Cook about 10 minutes, or until tender.

WILD ASPARAGUS WITH CHEDDAR CHEESE SAUCE

Scout out the wild asparagus sprouts by locating the old dead stalks from last season. Break off asparagus, taking only the tender shoots. Steam in an electric fry pan with water, butter and salt. Asparagus will be flat, so there's no need to tie into a bundle in a pot. Serve hot, pouring over the dish one can of hot, undiluted cheddar cheese soup.

LAYERED WILD GREEN SALAD

Gather enough tiny, tender violet leaves to equal small head of lettuce. Add one cup chopped wild onion tops (select the tiny tender ones known as wild chives); one cup young, shredded winter-cress leaves; one cup cleaned, chopped wild cucumber root; and one package of frozen peas, cooked according to directions on package. Layer vegetables, in order given, in a large glass bowl. Top with two cups of mayonnaise. (Do not mix mayonnaise, but let cover top of bowl to edge.)

Sprinkle three teaspoons sugar over mayonnaise. When ready to mix, you may add crumbled crisply fried bacon, Parmesan cheese, or chunks of cold, cooked wild meat.

WILD ONION – TOMATO BISCUITS

For my first wild dinner, I used elderberry blossom muffins, substituting one cup of blossoms in a blueberry muffin mix for the blueberries; but I add another idea that I developed when I was a youngster. I substituted tomato juice for the milk in my favorite biscuit recipe and then added one half cup of finely chopped wild onion tops — the tiny new tops, not the big ones.

REDBUD BLOSSOM JELLO

Add one cup of redbud blossoms and/or buds with one half cup chopped pecans to two boxes of prepared strawberry Jello. Buds float to top as Jello hardens. This will fill a shallow, 8 x 13 pan.

DANDELION JELLY

Gather enough dandelion blooms, pulling the yellow from the green heads, to make two cups. Boil water and pour four cups over blossoms. Let stand one half to one hour. When water is yellow, strain and measure out four cups of liquid. Using eight teaspoons of Surejell, two teaspoons lemon juice, five cups sugar, and a little yellow food coloring, make jelly according to jelly recipe on Surejell box. Pour hot jelly in sterilized jars, cap with hot paraffin and seal.

BLACKBERRY JAM CAKE

This is an easy cake to make after laboring so hard on the other parts of your wild meal. Mix one package of yellow cake mix with one half cup finely chopped hickory nuts, pecans or black walnuts, one fourth cup softened margarine, and one egg. Combine at low speed on mixer until crumbly. Press into a greased and floured 13 x 9 pan. Spread with one large jar of blackberry jam. (I heat the jam to make it spread more evenly.) Bake at 350 degrees for 20-25 minutes, or until edges are light brown. Make a glaze of one half cup powdered sugar, two and a half teaspoons water, and one half teaspoon almond extract. Drizzle this over warm cake. Cut into squares still warm.

The Greatest Show On Earth
by Joe Trembly

David Morgan, a circus enthusiast, reminisced about his boyhood experiences with the circus. He remembered the excitement in his hometown or Buckhannon, West Virginia. He recalled the preparations and the thrills upon the arrival of the "Big Top."

"As the red and gold boxcars rolled into town, excitement filled the air. The townspeople anxiously watched as the circus performers left the train. Each performer had a specific job to do in preparation for the afternoon show.

"Local boys would crowd around to see the acrobats, the clowns, and the elephants. Some boys became so involved with the circus atmosphere that they left home to follow the performers.

"Elephants and horses were used to set up the circus tents. The aroma of brewing coffee and frying eggs permeated the air. Tables and benches were set up, and the cover tent was raised over them. This tent became the cookhouse or mess hall.

" 'Hey Rube!' This phrase could be heard often when a worker needed help from another circus employee.

"Watching the construction of the 'Big Top' was an interesting experience. Two men would spot and start the stakes. Then, four large athletic-looking men with heavy driving hammers would stand at the four corners of the stake. Each man would strike the stake in rotation. Four or five swings from each man was sufficient to drive the stake.

"As the 'Big Top' was unloaded, it appeared as a mammoth bundle of canvas weighing over a ton, As it was unfolded, three or four center poles were set in place. Then the crews, assembled in various groups, grabbed the bull lines (ropes); instantly, it was up. Immediately, it was 'guyed' to the stakes. The several flags on the top were soon waving in the breeze; the tent seemed so large that it was almost frightening.

"As soon as the 'Big Top,' the menagerie or annex tent, and the electric power plant were ready for the first show, the circus performers dressed and prepared themselves for the street parade, a preview of the upcoming show. The gaily colored chariots and wagons bearing wild animals in cages were drawn through the streets by horses. Other animals included zebras, mounted camels, elephants, donkeys, and maybe even an ostrich pulling a sulky. Clowns brought great laughter as they led monkeys along the parade route.

"The circus band played tunes. Near the end of the parade, the big steam calliope could be heard whistling tunes like 'Over the Waves.'

"At the very end of the parade was the disgusted and shy clown with the wheelbarrow and scoop shovel.

"Shortly after the conclusion of the parade, tickets were sold for the first performance. Entering the grounds, visitors could pass through the menagerie or annex tent. Wild animals, snake charmers, the fat lady, and the fire eater might be seen.

"The shell game and the pea game operators would compete for customers among the spectators.

"Finally, the circus band began the theme song; the ringmaster climbed onto the stand in the center ring. He wore a bright swallow-tailed coat, a 'stove pipe' top hat, and carried a white cane. He started his introduction: 'Lad-ies and gentlemen, and those of you who sneaked in free.' The circus was underway.

"There were constant attractions in all three rings: bareback riding, stunts, juggling, tumbling, acrobats, trapeze artists, tightrope walkers, and trained animal acts. The specialty act was always performed in the center ring.

"The circus band was very important. Besides entertainment, it provided rhythm and timing for the acts. Sound effects were also created by the band.

"There was always the midway stretch period when the vendors would pass among the audience selling horrible-tasting boxed toffee or licorice candy which had a prize in every box — usually a snapping bug or a whistle. In every twenty-fifth box, there was supposed to be a $5.00 bill. 'This could be the one!' The vendors also sold pop, peanuts, popcorn, Cracker Jacks, and circus souvenirs.

"The most amazing aspect of the circus was the clowns. There were three types of clowns. The 'Charlie' clown was funny in a sad sort of way, but he always brought laughter. The 'Joey' clown was the 'do-all' clown. He could do anything that the regular performers could do. He could even perform better sometimes. He blundered and fell a few times. The 'General' clown wore a funny 'make-up' nose and big shoes. He was always bumping into people and objects.

"The grand finale was the ending of the main attraction and usually a review of the show's highlights.

"As the night performance ended, the tear-down operations began. The 'Big Top' would likely be falling down as the spectators left. The circus would be on its way to the next town.

"Today, the circus has lost much of its glamour. It travels by truck instead of by train. Due to traffic problems, there is almost never a parade.

"Only a few circuses survive today. In 1946, there were 45 circuses traveling in the United States and appearing under canvas. In 1952, there were 28; today, there is only about 9. In 1946 there were only 9 indoor circuses; today there are about 29.

"Today the circus needs a great deal of promotion. Many smaller circuses have become a part of an organized charity in order to survive.

"The idea of the circus goes back to the ancient Romans. The word **circus** stems from the circular arenas built by the Romans to stage chariot races, battles between men and beasts, and other forms of entertainment. The oldest known circus was Circus Maximus in Rome in 326 B.C.

"The first circus in the United States dates back to 1793, a production sponsored by John William Ricketts in Philadelphia. The show included fancy riding, a tightrope walker, and a clown and was attended by President George Washington.

"The symbol of the American circus — the elephant — arrived three years later (1796) from India. The audience was delighted as it watched the elephant remove corks from bottles with the end of its trunk.

"The golden age of the circus in the United States was a 90 year period which lasted from 1850 to 1940. Elaborate menageries were added in the 1850's to avoid criticism that the shows were immoral. The traveling zoos were added to make the circus look more educational.

"In the early years of this century, the big circuses competed vigorously for customers. In the dead of the winter, the advance men were out buying advertisement space on barns and buildings to 'ballyhoo' the shows for the following summer. One poster war became so intense that within a few days barns and billboards in choice areas were covered with layers of flamboyant pictures.

"The competition also extended to feature attractions. One circus had a genuine albino elephant. A competitor tried to go one better by whitewashing an elephant to make him whiter than the albino. The fraud was exposed when a cloudburst washed off the whitewash.

"In the 1930's, there were large scale mergers which led to Ringling Brothers and Barnum and Bailey. It became the largest of the tent shows. But, like most of the others, it no longer travels with a tent. It plays only in auditoriums.

"The circuses have changed. But, they probably will be with us as long as children enjoy animals, clowns, and men and women on the flying trapeze.

HITCHING ALLEY

"Before the days of the automobile, hitching alleys for the horses were a common sight in our cities; Buckhannon, West Virginia was no exception. The hitching alley in Buckhannon was adjacent to the circus grounds near the rear of Shannon's Hardware Store. It was well-equipped with post and hitching rails for the convenience of the citizens who commuted by horseback, rigs, surreys, or wagons.

"On one circus day, the alley was filled to capacity, and the nearness of the circus grounds caused uneasiness among the horses and mules. The scent of the wild animals, the roaring of the lions, and the noises of strange animals upset the horses.

"When the 'Big Top' went up, it startled the horses and mules, and many of them jerked away from the hitching rail and were off and running. It was like a chain reaction, and wild disorder and confusion were created. Some of the horses slipped their halters and bridles, or broke ropes and hitching straps. They stampeded wildly through town. Even the most dependable and gentle 'old plugs' ran wildly, some as far as the college campus before being caught."

Roy Murphy

Mr. Roy Murphy devoted his entire life to the big shows until paralysis in his legs forced him to retire. This setback has not dampened his love or respect for the circus.

"I graduated from high school out here back in the Great Depression. There wasn't no work, and I didn't like loafin' around. I had several little part-time jobs at unloadin' cement and working behind the cement mixer. I think I only got maybe a half a day or a day's work in every month or two. So then the circus come along, and I joined it because it gave me employment. I was out to the circus grounds in the Stephenson Field. They was short on help. I talked to the boss and he said, 'Start to work in the morning. Go home and get your clothes and come back and take in the circus tonight.' That's the way I joined the Sam B. Dils Show. It was a big one; we had 123 trucks and trailers. Beautiful show, all new canvas, nice menagerie, and everything.

"I was with the concession department when I first went on the circus. My job was a cashier's job, and I had the big menagerie candy stand. That's where you go in the menagerie, and there's about six boys who would wait on you: Cracker Jacks, cold drinks, peanuts, novelties, and candy bars. Then, while the show was going on, I had to check the boys that came in and sold popcorn and Cracker Jacks in the stands. After the show was over, I used half of those boys to pick up pop bottles, and the other half had to sack the peanuts. Then we'd come back and get ready for the night show. In the night show we would do the same thing all over again. About halfway through the show we would tear down, or have torn down, the menagerie candy stand and load them up. We would help pull the stakes on the 'Big Top' after the show was over.

"If it was a railroad show, we would walk maybe a mile, two miles, down to the train, what we call the runs, where we had our quarters. There was no air conditioning, and everybody would set out along the track until the train started to move. When the train started to move, we'd jump up and go in and sleep goin' from one town to the next. Each sleeping car had a car porter that made up the beds and put clean sheets on and so forth. He'd shine your shoes and even come through the car and say, 'Twenty miles from town — ev'rybody up!' Everybody had to get up and get dressed because when that train stopped, if you wasn't ready to work, you was fined two dollars.

"Then we would walk to the circus grounds; sometimes it was three or four blocks. Sometimes it might be a couple or three miles clear across town. When we got to the circus grounds, we had to put up the menagerie. I would hire about 10 boys and give 'em free passes to help. We would get the menagerie up; then I would turn the 10 boys loose with their passes and take my regular gang of concession men and unload our wagon, put up our tents, and get ready to sell peanuts, popcorn, and everything on the outside. (Sometimes we had to go out and walk down the parade route to the circus grounds sellin' balloons, books, and birdies-on-a-stick.) We would go eat and get ready to work the afternoon show. Our days was usually — oh — maybe six or seven in the morning till twelve or one o'clock at night. A lot of times, we would see the sun come up the next day.

"Some of the wagons wheels was almost buried in the mud when it would rain. They'd have to hitch two eight-horse hitches, eight horses in each hitch, you know, on the front. They might have a couple of elephants pushin' 'em in the back. They'd get 'em (circus equipment) off the lot by a lot of hard work.

"I can remember, we come out of Anniston, Alabama, (think it mighta been '33, '34—somewhere in there) and went over to Birmingham an' was in there two days for the Shrine. From Birmingham it started to rain the second night, and we never saw the sunshine until we got to Scranton, Pennsylvania, 44 days later. Almost every night we would work until daylight the next morning, and the only sleep we had was goin' from one town to the next. A **LOT** of hard work, and it seemed you never got enough rest, y'know, or got enough sleep.

"It was easier to work on a big truck show than it was on a railroad show because on a truck show, your sleeping trailer was there. When you got through working at night, you walked into the sleeping trailer and went to bed. On a big railroad show, sometimes you had to walk two or three miles across town. You was already tired out, wore out, and fatigued; then you had that **long** walk back to the runs. We got quite a bit more rest on the big truck show.

"That was the life of a concession man on the circuses. Work, work, work, and then more work. I've been in every state in the United States and some of those states for months at a time."

WINTER QUARTERS

"For the wintertime, long about the middle of October, we went into winter quarters and wasn't on the road. We put everything in winter quarters some place in the South because those animals got pneumonia the same as the people did. We had to get 'em out of cold weather and keep 'em out of cold weather. We would open the season about the first of May. The Ringling show used to winter in Indiana and Wisconsin, and they never broke winter quarters until the first of May."

TROUBLE SHOOTING

"Later, I was what they call a 'Trouble-shooter' on the show. On every big circus, there's a person around that will take care of any eventuality. No matter what kind of trouble comes up on that show, some person there was able to take care of it. I used to take care of quite a few of 'em. We had a blow down; strong gusts of wind about 50-75 miles an hour could blow down the 'Big Top.' I would go into the menagerie and drop the menagerie to save the tent. Once as I dropped the last pole, (there was five poles about 350-60 feet long). I run over and dove under a wagon to keep from gettin' killed. I dropped that 'Big Top' right on those cages to save that top and those animals.

"I had to check the shows in and out of different states. These states in the West had what they call 'Ports of Entry,' and every truck that went into that state had to stop and turn in their papers and have those papers checked.

"Another one of my jobs was, I remember, I had to go into a town at 2:00 in the morning; the circus ground wasn't nothin' but a big dump — tin cans they'd been pilin' five and six feet high. I had to hire a couple of bulldozers to level off that dump so that the show could be put up there when it arrived the next morning at six or seven o'clock. Any kind of trouble that the show had, I had to take care of it.

"We used to get roughnecks once in a while that came on the circus grounds. I would send the police out to run 'em off of the lot. Sometimes they'd fight, but when we went after the police, they wouldn't fight too much. Usually we'd put a couple of chains on an elephant's trunk; (the elephants would swing the chains) and that was all there was to it — we wouldn't mess with them. I'd run that elephant right up the center of 'em and bring her back; that was all she wrote.

"On top of that, they'd send me out of town maybe two or three days ahead of the circus to take care of some kind of trouble. Maybe if someone stole a pony or something, I had to stay behind for a day or two to find that pony and get it back on the show. I mean, I had all that trouble to deal with."

JOBS

"Everybody in the circus had a job to do, and they done it just as quick as possible and then got away from it. If some person didn't do their job, somebody else would have to do it for them. If it was a case of sickness or illness, well then, the man was excused until he felt better and went back to work. When it was a case of laziness, he was shown the highway and told that that road went two directions, up and down. He could take his choice. They didn't want to see him on the show no more. It was rough, but you had to do your work.

"On the circus staff you usually have the owner and the manager.

The manager usually takes care of the marquee and the people comin' in the circus—he'll take their tickets. Then the next in line to the manager is the agent. a lot of times the agent can go to as many as two or three towns and won't get a booking. For that reason, they usually start out in January, February, months or weeks before the circus starts out. They will route that circus from the time it leaves the barn in the springtime till it gets back in the wintertime. The agent's job is to get the lot wherever it's gonna show and to find out about the city license. Then he usually hires maybe four, five, or six policemen to keep order in the crowds. After he books the town for the circus to perform in, he will send the information back to the circus owner.

"Two weeks before that circus goes on the road, the brigade will go out. Now the brigade is a gang of men that does the advertising. works on the billboards up against the buildings, and puts the signs and the showcards in the windows. And one day before the circus leaves winter headquarters, there's another man that goes out—the 24-hour man. This 24-hour man does all the buying—anything that circus has got to have, that 24-hour man will buy it. There's food for the animals, for the people, and any kind of hardware.

"The superintendent is the man that runs the show. I had a friend: he was superintendent on the circus. We was traveling out in the West, and we come to a river where the bridge was washed out. He just unloaded the big poles and threw some stringers (Stringers looked like they was cut out of stair steps; they put the platforms and seats on 'em,) and moved that circus across that river. If he didn't get them across, he had, I think, 88 miles to detour around. They was 15 minutes late getting the afternoon show started. If he hadn't've done that, they wouldn't've had no afternoon show that time.

"The superintendent walks around and supervises the departments. There's a stake and chain department, canvas, seat, side show, and electric departments. He makes sure that he has bosses for each department. These bosses had to see that the work is done. To see that everything is unloaded and put up is also the superintendent's job. Each department takes care of their own end of putting up, taking down, and working on that circus.

"When the show gets in town, there's a man called a lay-out man. He is the architect of that show; he measures those lots off. Those shows usually take about 10-15 acres in tents. He's got all the small, big, and different size tents. In different towns, the lots would be altogether different; the lot that he measures off and lays out today, he couldn't measure out tomorrow.

"Early of a morning when the circus moves to a new town, there'll be two men who start out from the circus and go to the next town ahead of all the rest of that show. They will put arrows on crossroads and different streets. Those arrows is what we call reels. We'd follow those arrows when we'd go through strange towns; maybe there's a hundred turnoffs. We'd follow the markings and get out on the lot with no trouble.

"Also the circus has welders, blacksmiths, and somebody around able to take care of those types of problems."

"SAINTS AND SINNERS"

"Circus people usually stayed with the circus the whole year. The shows all gave bonuses. If you stayed till the end of the season, you get a bonus. For that reason, when they signed up for those shows, they stayed the whole season. There was some people come and stay for a while and then leave ... they was known as circus 'Saints and Sinners.' These circus 'Saints and Sinners' was bankers, lawyers, doctors, dentists, and big merchants, most of them very very wealthy. They'd come on the circus and stay for a week, two weeks, a month, maybe two or three months. They did it because they loved the circus. There is a dentist up at Marietta that's a circus 'Saint and Sinner.' Their motto is, 'Anything to help the circus or circus person.' For example, say I get in trouble and put in jail, we got some lawyers down there to get me out.

"In almost every town you'll have some of these lawyers, doctors, wealthy businessmen, and bankers; and they'd help the circus."

TERMITE

"On every circus there's somebody that impressed me quite a bit. Joey Myers was a wonderful acrobat. She worked three or four acts besides the high act and the trapeze act. She was a very good person.

"Then there was this little five year old boy we called 'Termite.' His father was the lion tamer, wild animal act. The boy was the bookkeeper. Five years old and he was keeping his dad's books! One day he says 'Where you goin'?

"I said, 'I'm going down to the town to get a ice cream sundae.'

"He said, 'Can I go with you?'

"I said, 'Get your dad to let me know.' So he went over and his father held up his hand, 'OK.' We went down to the delicatessen. He got a banana split, and I got a ice cream sundae. We had a twenty dollar bill and when we got ready to leave, he gave the woman twenty dollars. She short-changed him a dollar.

"He said, 'Lady, you didn't give me enough money. You count that again.'

"She counted it and said, 'No, I made a mistake. Why aren't you in school?'

"He said, 'I don't go to school; I'm only five years old.' Now, that kid sold tickets on the side show, handled any kind of change, ten, twenty dollars, I don't care what it was! Of a night when the show was over, that kid would have a bucket of pennies, dimes, and nickels. He would put that money in wrappers, count it out and put it down in the books.

"I used to turn in tickets to him and he'd say, 'You owe me $231.00.' I'd count him out the $231.00. He would recount it and was doin' that since he was four years old.

"But it tickled the hell out of me when he told that woman, 'I'm only five years old!'"

DINNER-HOUSE

A circus dinner house is in two departments — what they called the long side and the short side. On the long side, the workingmen eat. On the short side, your performers, your concession people, and your staff eat. We would all go eat when th' flag was up. (When the meal was ready, they would raise a flag.) Nobody eats when th' flag isn't up.

There's a table for each department, and they have their own waiter that served that table. In the middle of the table, we had all kinds of jams, jellies, relishes, ketchups, and all kind of cereals. If you wanted a dry cereal for breakfast, you helped yourself; there was enough on the table. Then the waiter would bring hot cakes, sausage, bacon, eggs, and potatoes. Well, they made a pretty fair meal. Occasionally, there'd be doughnuts or something like that.

"Noontime, it was changed a little bit; we got meat, mashed potatoes, gravy, a dessert, a salad, and two vegetables. You could have as much as you wanted except dessert; you had one dessert. You could order seconds, thirds, fourths; there was no limit.

"In the evening, it was about the same thing. If you had roast beef for lunch, for evening you might have pork chops, maybe baked potatoes, or always something different.

"In the kitchen there was a salad boy, the chef, and the cook; they'd furnish meals for maybe three, four, five, or six hundred people, whatever was on that show. Just the three of them did all that work! Circus food is equal to anything they have here or up to the local restaurant. As soon as they see you come in, they start bringing your food.

"The waiters would have to peel potatoes, wash potatoes, or skin 'em. After the potatoes was washed, they'd put 'em in a steel drum and turn the steam on 'em. You'd have to cook them 30-40 minutes with the jackets on, but now, three minutes and they was cooked. To fry bacon, they'd throw 10 or 12 pounds of bacon in a big pan two or three feet long and a couple of feet wide. When it comes out, it'll unwrinkle and it's in pretty good shape. That is the way they would prepard meals for the circus hands."

SHRINE CIRCUS

"There is a Shrine Circus that comes here to Parkersburg now, and there's no comparison between that show and the ones that I was with. You have good acts, but they don't have that 'Big Top' that has to go up and down. You see, on those big shows, we had five or ten acres of tents. In those acres, we might have 40 or 50 smaller tents besides the big ones. We had the dressing rooms, too; they was tents. You call them tents, we call them 'rags.' "

FAMILY

"The circus people are different; they're a strict family group. Carnival people and circus people are an altogether different breed of people, but they help one another out. It's all show business. I can remember one time we was unloading the circus and there was a big carnival on that run. Those wagons was buried in the mud. So I told Curly to take a couple of elephants in there and push those damn wagons out of there so that we could get in. Help 'em out y'know.

Louise Butcher, Teacher at Spruce
by Brenda Goddard and Brenda Henline

Louise Butcher started her teaching career at the mountaintop town of Spruce, West Virginia. At one time Spruce was the highest city in the United States. There were no roads up the mountain to this rich lumber area; and to get there, you had to own your own motorcar that ran on the railroad tracks or ride the Shay engine up from the town of Cass, West Virginia. Mrs. Butcher describes her first trip up the mountain and her year on the mountain as a one-room school teacher.

"The first morning that I was to report to school to work, I didn't know what I was going to ride. I knew I was going to ride a train, but I didn't know what kind of train. It was raining, and I had a raincoat. I think it was white. When I got there the engineer said, 'You can't wear that.' I said, 'Well, it's all I have.' So, Clarence took his shirt off and gave it to me.

"The train that I was going to ride was the 'Old' Shay engine that brought the logs off of the mountain. Of course, there wasn't any cars for passengers, you had to ride right up in the cab. I got in there, and there was a little box where the engineer sits. He said, "If you'd like to, you can sit down there." Well, I sat down there. By the time I got to Spruce, my hands, face and hair were black. And as I say, it was raining. That first morning when we got up to the switch-back, I thought, 'What on earth are they doing now?' I didn't know what a switchback was. (The trains go so far up the mountain and level off and then reverse up the next section of the mountain. By using this zigzag method, they are able to climb the steep sections of the mountain.)

"After that first morning, I learned not to sit on that box. I stood up after that. All of that stuff from the smokestack just fell on my head. That morning was the first time that I had ever been to Spruce. All of the houses were black. They didn't have a bit of paint on them.

"I think we left Cass about four o'clock in the morning, so it was about five o'clock when we arrived. I think it took about an hour to get up there. Anyway, it wasn't daylight. That was on a Monday morning. I had to go back (off the mountain) for supplies at the middle of the week. I thought, well, I'll stay until the middle of the week; and when I go for supplies, I won't go back. But, you know, when the time came to go, I was ready to go back.

"When I arrived that first morning, nobody was up. They knew somebody was coming to teach, but everybody was in bed. So, the trainmaster said he would take me down to the place that always kept the teacher. Well, when we got to the house, they were all in bed. We finally got them up.

"When I was at Spruce, there wasn't much there. They had a boarding house, but it wasn't running when I was there. They didn't even have a store up there. Just before that they had a store, but it and the boarding house had both closed. There was nothing there. Most of the houses were built alike. They were weatherboarded and unpainted. The houses where I stayed had three rooms downstairs, a living room, kitchen, and I guess a dining room. then, upstairs they had three bedrooms.

"It was so cold in those houses. They had a stove in the kitchen and a stove in the living room. I think maybe they had a register in one of the upstairs bedrooms to let the heat up. It was so cold of a morning that ice would be frozen over the windows; I mean on the inside. When I would get up there on Monday mornings, I would just go to bed with my snow suit on to keep warm (until time for school to start). After, I learned how to dress — I didn't wear a white coat after the first morning. It was really some experience.

"The school was a two room building, but we just had one room going when I was there. I taught all the grades; however, there was a few grades that no students were in. There were boys in the seventh and eighth trade that were bigger than I was.

"The houses at Spruce were in two rows. Some were off, but the most were in rows. They had boardwalks to walk on. There was a main walk and then walks branched off into each house. The boarding house was the biggest building. All of the buildings were two story, but it was the largest building. There was the rows of houses, and then the schoolhouse was away from them. It was kind of up on the bank. At one time, it had been a nice building. It had two big rooms. So, at one time, they had a lot more students."

WEEKENDS

"I went home every weekend. So, on Monday mornings I'd drive my car over to Cass and leave my car at the mill. One of the workers there would take it back home for me. then I'd walk up the track and wait at the water tank in the lumberyard for the train. One morning some of the men said, 'Why don't you come up here?' They had a little house (dog house) that had a stove in it where they waited. So, they said, 'Come on up where it is warm.' I didn't know how many men were in there. So, I thought, if they ask me to, I will. I went up there and walked in and all of those men were around this stove; and when I walked in, they all stopped talking and nobody said a word. So, I thought I'd better not do that again. I am putting a damper on something. So, from then on, I just waited at the water tank.

"I wasn't supposed to be riding the train. The trainmaster said something about they couldn't let anybody that was under age. He told me I could ride for a few times. then he told the men one morning that they could take me that week — up on Monday and back on Friday, but that was the last.

"The men (on the train) were real nice and they said, 'If your daughter was teaching school up there and standing out here for a ride, wouldn't you want us to take her up?' They said, 'We are going to pick her up just as long as she is there.' Something happened; he lost his job, or I guess I couldn't have ridden. There was no way up or down, and I would have had to stay up there. If I would have had to spend a weekend up there, I would have thought I was ruined. I came home every Friday evening.

"The snows were deep, and it was windy up there. The snows drifted, and they had to keep a path shoveled to the school for us to walk on. There wasn't any time we couldn't get to school. You know, I never missed a day up there. If I had been sick, I guess there would have been a holiday.

"I remember two first graders that I had, two little twin girls. Those little kids memorized. There was a long bench in front of the room, and you brought each class up there to have their classes. I remember these little girls were up there, and this one was reading, and it was the next one's turn. She was looking out the window, and she just took it up where the other one left off and read and didn't even look at her book. She had memorized the story.

"In the winter, everybody ice-skated on a pond up there for entertainment. They sat around and talked. There was no modern conveniences, no electricity in the houses; they had oil lamps and an outside 'john.' It sat away out and had a boardwalk to get to it also. It had big cracks in the walls. Snow would blow. It makes me shiver to think about it now. I'd freeze to death now if I had to go up there. But then I didn't think anything about it.

"A child was paid to fire the pot-bellied stove at the school. They would go earlier and have the school warm for us. Everyone went home for lunch. They all lived right there.

"Nobody came to see me. The superintendent didn't come. Nobody came but some insurance salesman one time the whole year. That was the only person that came to the school that year. I have often thought about that. A new person starting out like that, and nobody came to see what I was doing or how I was doing.

"A lot of times a motorcar would come to Cass earlier than the train on Friday afternoon, and they (school officials) told me that I could come anytime on Friday afternoon off the mountain. One time I was on one of the motorcars and it had sleeted and the tracks were covered with ice. the brakes wouldn't hold anything; we got home.

"For a long time I couldn't tell the difference between the 'Old" Shay engine and the Western Maryland train. Of course, there was a big difference. The kids could tell the difference, and they would hear the train coming, and they would tell me the Shay's coming on Friday afternoon. they knew they were going to get out of school it it was two o'clock, two-thirty or no matter what time it was.

"There was always one of the parents that would walk down to the train with me and carry my suitcase. When the men (on the train) would see me standing out there, they would always stop to get me.

"Those people really appreciated everything you did for them. It's really not like today. They had no store or anything, and when they needed something they had to go to Cass or Mace on a motorcar, if they had one, to get groceries or whatever they needed. A lot of them had motorcars to travel on. They would get out maybe once a week or maybe not that often. They'd bring me a list of things to buy for them when I came off the mountain on Fridays. I have bought everything from baby powder to oranges to I don't know what all. I would just pack my suitcases full with things they wanted.

"Those people weren't there for a lifetime. They were just there with the company. They were real good people. They knew they wouldn't be there forever. I just taught there for one year. The next year I came down to Cass to teach.

"They finally tore all of those houses down at Spruce. There is not a building standing up there. Today, you can go up there on the Cass Scenic Railroad. We went up there on the train, and I didn't even recognize it now. The only thing there now is some foundations. It looks completely different."

Flint Erving and Stoner Lumber Co.'s Mill — Picture loaned by Susan Monk.

Making Swiss Cheese
by Russ Fornash and Jeff Roberts

The Ballie sisters live in the white frame farmhouse where they were born. The house was built by their father on the farm next to the one settled by Christian Ballie, their grandfather.

Christian Ballie came to the mountains of Webster County, West Virginia, on a promise from a land agent that the area would remind him of his native home in the Swiss Alps.

The farm encompasses 218 acres of beautiful mountain terrain. They presently have four cows that require milking morning and evening, some stock cattle, pigs, chickens, and a couple of collie dogs.

The sisters arise each morning at daybreak to milk the cows and start the farm chores. While Anna and Freda are busy milking, Gertrude tends to the household chores; she prepares the milk for the cheese-making process and a warm cup of tea for all to relax and enjoy.

FAMILY

"Our father and his brother built this house that we live in 1903 or 1904. All of the wood inside (walls) are tongue-and grooved by hand.

"Our parents only spoke Swiss when they came here. Our mother was born in Switzerland and came to this country when she was just a baby. Our father was born in America, in Ohio. Then he

Freda, salting the cheese.

Anna, Gertrude and Freda Ballie.

moved to this area. It was mostly Swiss people that settled this area (Webster County, West Virginia). We don't know when mother and father started speaking English. We still speak Swiss around the house. We learned to speak English in school.

"We girls used to mow all of this territory with the horses. Now we use a tractor. We got it when we were older, and we were afraid to learn (to operate it). So, we have a neighbor up here, and he comes down and drives the machinery for us.

"We only have four cows that we milk now. Last fall, we had nine cows to milk and make cheese from. We also have stock cattle that we keep on the farm. We also keep a couple of hogs that we butcher. We usually butcher in the spring, the last of March or the first of April. Then we have to freeze the meat; but if you butcher in the fall, you can cure the meat."

TO MAKE CHEESE

"To make the cheese, we use evening and morning milk. The evening milk sets until morning; then we take the cream off. Then we put the morning milk in whole. We have Jersey and Guernsey

Freda taking cheese from the mold.

cows, so we take the cream out. Some people use the cream, but they have Holsteins. If you are making Limburg cheese, you put all of the cream in.

"We don't make cheese during the wintertime. We turn the cows dry (late fall). There is a difference in the cheese when the cows are eating hay and grain than there is in the summer when they eat green grass. In the winter the cheese stays a whiter color than in the summertime. The cheese won't hardly ripen in the winter when it is cold. It ripens better when it is warm.

"When you take the cheese out of the press, it is real white. As it gets riper, it gets yellower. Some people like it older, and some like it kind of young. In fact, there is a lady that comes here every summer, and she wants to buy the cheese that is only a week old. They like it best that way.

"You need it in a warmer place to ripen. We keep it in our basement. Our basement is kind of cold in the winter, and the cheese won't hardly ripen.

"If the cheese gets too old, it gets hard. It gets too hard to eat. Usually, we can keep it about two months or so. We kept it all winter when Mom and Dad were living, because they would put paraffin wax around it. That will preserve the moisture in it."

RECIPE

The following is the Ballie sisters' secret to making excellent Swiss Cheese:

SWISS CHEESE

6 gallons milk (milk with part cream — some cream skimmed out)
1 gallon whole milk

Heat the milk (in cold packer) until it comes up to 86 degrees.

Put ¾ tablet cheese rennet in one glass cold water to dissolve.

After it dissolves, pour into milk after the milk has been heated to 86 degrees.

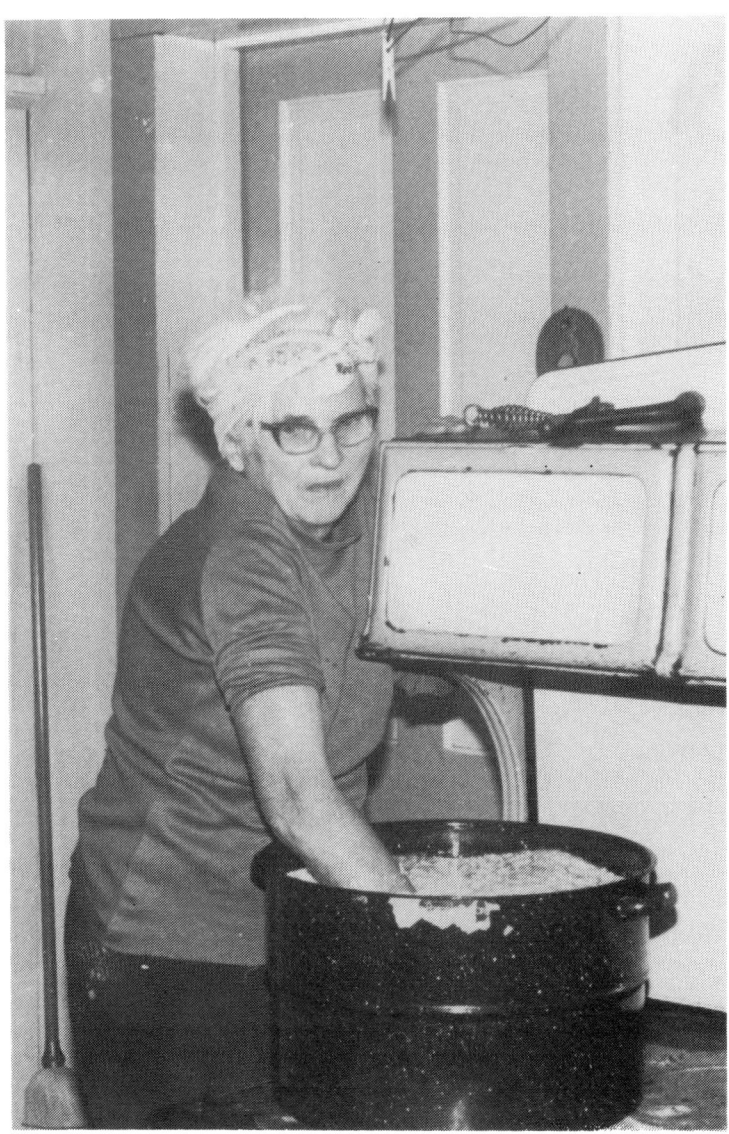

Gertrude making Swiss cheese.

Stir the rennet into the milk (with your hands).

Let the milk, with the rennet, sit for one hour (until good and clabber).

Put the milk on the stove again and heat slowly until it comes to 106 degrees. Stir constantly.

Take it off the stove and let it set for another hour.

Pour the whey off.

Before putting the cheese clabber in the press, put cheesecloth in the press.

Pat the clabber into the cheese press. It stays in the press with the cloth for about one hour.

Take the cheese and cloth out of the press.

Leave the cloth out, but put the cheese back in the press until evening.

After you put the cheese back into the press, you have to tighten the press every little bit.

Take the cheese out and put it in the basement in the evening.

Put a pinch of salt on it every other day for five days and rub it in (salt flavors it).

Wash the cheese before rubbing the salt in (takes the mold off).

Turn the cheese every day. (This lets air to the cheese.)

As the cheese ages, it turns yellow.

CHEESE SHOULD BE COOKED ON A WOOD BURNING STOVE FOR BETTER FLAVOR

Streetcars of Parkersburg and Marietta
by Mark Nesselroad and Jeff Roberts

The Park City Railway Company was incorporated in 1888. It built and operated a horse-drawn streetcar service in Parkersburg. The actual operation of the business began in 1889.

A group of local businessmen proposed that the city install an electric cable car system in 1897. This system would replace the horse-drawn streetcar. The city council granted a franchise to the Parkersburg Gas, Electric Light, and Street Railway Company. However, the horse-drawn cars continued to operate until the new system was finished.

In 1898, the company began construction of two new lines. The inner loop traveled along Spring, Gould, and Lynn Streets. The outer loop went from Gould Street to City Park. These lines opened on July 2, 1898. The cars on the inner loop were painted green; the ones on the outer loop were red. Six months later, additional cars were added due to the number of passengers.

The decision was made in 1899 to add an additional track between Parkersburg and Williamstown. However, because of the bad weather, the track wasn't finished being graded until 1901. A power plant was built in Williamstown to run the streetcars. The streetcar company arranged for the building of a bridge between Williamstown and Marietta, Ohio.

The streetcar companies of Marietta and Parkersburg consolidated in 1902 to form the Parkersburg Marietta and Interurban Railway Company. Hourly streetcar service was then provided to Williamstown. The bridge to Marietta was completed in 1903, and a regular run started between Parkersburg and Williamstown. It was decided in 1908 that another streetcar line would be constructed along the Muskingum River in Ohio from Marietta. The tracks were run to Lowell, Ohio; later, they were built on into Beverly, Ohio. The end of the streetcar line was in Beverly. Farmers used this run to ship produce to the market; the track was said to have carried more produce than passengers.

Tracks were built in 1908 that ran from South Parkersburg to the Wood County Fairgrounds. This line became known as the Viscose Line. A track to Murdoch Avenue and a loop in the north end of Parkersburg were added later.

With the coming of the automobile, trucks, and better roads, the streetcar service began to decline. The freight service ended in the 1920's. The Beverly line folded in 1929, and the Marietta City Lines closed in 1934.

On November 1, 1944, the streetcars in Parkersburg were purchased by the City Lines of West Virginia. The north end run was closed on November 26, 1946. The Marietta interurban stopped on April 12, 1947. The Viscose and south side streetcar line ended on May 25, 1947. This had been the last working line in Parkersburg. After closing down the streetcar service, the City Lines Company provided a city bus service in Parkersburg until August 27, 1969

NOBEL SCHOFIELD

Nobel Schofield is a retired streetcar operator. He recalls many events of the early days.

"In numbering the cars, the first number was the type and the other two numbers were an identification number. The number 317, 319, or 324 was one type of car. That's what we called the 300 series. The 800's were another type, and the 600's were another type.

"The 600's all had manual operated doors. The rest of the cars' doors were air operated.

"The amount of time to stop one of the cars depended on the car. The 600's had big wheels like a railroad coach, and it took a little time to get them stopped.

"The 300's were definitely city cars. They would probably go about 35 miles an hour.

Mark Nesselroad, Nobel Schofield and Jeff Roberts look at old streetcar pictures.

"We had the distinction of having the only 800's ever built. They were a pain in the neck, in one way. They had little motors, but they were high speed motors. The motors were low, and if you had three puddles in a row, the motors would stop running. If someone threw a brick down in the middle of the street, you had a motor on it, and you was off the track. Their motors were kind of round; if you hit something, they would just pop up and the wheels would go off (the track). If the wheels were off the track a couple of inches, you were out of business.

"Most of the old cars had what they called a cow catcher. It was a big thing that was supposed to just plow things off the road.

"But on the cars we had had two wooden bars. If they hit anything, they would fly up and a carriage would drop down behind them; it would pick anything up. It dropped down like a shovel. Then the driver had to get out and remove it. This kept the wheels and motors from going over it.

"Then after you got the object out, you raised the carriage up again with your foot inside. The pedal would fly up when the carriage went down. You shoved it back down, and that raised the carriage back up and latched it."

RUNS

"The first run was out of the barn at 4:45 a.m. People used to depend were stored at night or repaired) at 4:35 a.m. People used to depend on the streetcars to go to work. That meant that we had to be at the barn ten minutes before your turn, or they got somebody else to run the streetcar. That is what we called report time. The last streetcar came in at 1:35 at night. Everything connected with the streetcars had two shifts, but the barn men and they had three shifts. The barn men only worked eight hours. My turn, that I worked for years, was nine hours and thirty-five minutes — no overtime, ever. The span between 4:35 a.m. and 1:35 a.m. was divided equally into two parts among the operators.

"We had four regular cars running to Marietta, three regular cars running to south side, and four regular cars running on Park Avenue. A lot of people depended on them. The run to the Viscose, or other plants, was what we called the extra board. Soon after the Viscose started, they staggered their shifts; some shifts ended at 3:00,

4:00, and 5:00 o'clock. But before they started staggering the shifts, I have seen nine carloads of people down there to be hauled.

"We had twelve minute service here in north end with the four cars running. You had forty-eight minutes to run from Third and Juliana Streets and back to Third and Juliana.

"When we ran to Williamstown and Marietta on the interurban, we had to run on train orders. We had a dispatcher that gave you orders where to wait on a switch so two streetcars could pass. He would tell you where to go and when not to go. In town, the switches had lights on a pole, so you would know if another streetcar was coming and to wait on it."

INTERIOR OF STREETCAR

"The streetcars that ran in town had wooden seats, slats of wood. They were comfortable enough for city riding.

"The ones that run on the interurban to Marietta had leather seats in them. They were really grand. Then, instead of having the long seat in front, it had a single bucket seat. They were very comfortable. Two people could sit on each side of the aisle that ran down the center.

"Most of the cars would hold about forty-eight passengers sitting. I remember one time I was downtown, and it come up a rain. It

317 car used for passengers in Parkersburg — Picture loaned by Nobel Schofield.

was around 4:00 p.m. Some of the plants were just letting out, and I came out of town with a 300 car with 138 passengers."

FARE

"Back when I was a kid and until World War I, the fare was a nickel. From stop to stop, it was a nickel. From Parkersburg to Marietta, it was twenty-five cents. From Williamstown to Marietta, it was a nickel. Then they raised it to seven cents, and thirty-five cents to Marietta. It was a flat seven cents, no variation."

ACCIDENTS

"There were some accidents. The streetcars killed the tollkeeper on the East Street Bridge. He stepped out in front of it.
"There was another man, I remember, that was killed on Seventh Street at the end of Harris Street. Every once in a while, they tore up an automobile. Somebody would pull across in front of them. I hit a milk truck over on the intersection of Camden and Hickory Streets, but nobody got hurt.
"Another time I was driving the work car, and it didn't have an automatic control on it. Consequently, we had to have a brakeman ride on the cinder car. In case it broke loose, he could hand brake it. We was going on the interurban, and I had the track boss with me. It started to rain a little bit, and there was a platform for the brakeman to ride on. He had squatted down on the platform so the rain would go over his head. The track boss was riding in the cab with me and happed to glance back and couldn't see the brakeman. I don't know what gave him the idea, but he just opened the door and swung out to see what happened to the brakeman. Just then, we went into the Boaz Bridge. The door hit the bridge, and fortunately, it hit his shoulder first and not his head, or it would have split his head down. That is the only reason he lived and wasn't killed. That was the only accident that I ever had that injured anyone."

SNOW/ICE

"Your problem with snow and ice wasn't on the track, but on the wire. The wire would ice over, and you would just, more or less, melt it off with resistance. The fire would fly, and you

The 700 car was a line car. It had a top like an elevator so the men could work on the line.

The 652 was more or less a locomotove. It could pull cars, or work the track. It pulled flat cars that hauled the rails.

could burn up a trolley wheel fast. We had what they called sleet cutters. The sleet cutter was a brass cast, V-shaped object that was pointed. It ran in front of the trolley wheel on the wire and cut the ice off the wire. But, if you forgot and reversed your car, you cut the line in two, period.

"The last year we ran the streetcars was after the war, and we had an ice storm. They wouldn't let us put the sleet cutters on because wire was still scarce, and you couldn't get wire. There just wasn't any wire available. We had to run the cars without the cutters on the wheel, and I am telling you, that the fire was flying just like an electric welder. It would just cut the trolley wheels in two. The only thing you could do was call the barn man, and he would come down and put a new trolley wheel on. Then you'd ride it for a while; and the first thing you knew, it would go flying off. They still wouldn't let us put the sleet cutters on. We really had a pain in the neck that winter.

Eric Ruff, Earl Booth and Ken Gilbert look at Earl's streetcar hat.

EARL BOOTH

Earl Booth operated streetcars in Parkersburg and remembers a variety of exciting times during his tenure.

"When you started on the streetcars, they put you with an experienced operator. The place you normally went to break in was the north end run, and they usually gave you a 300 car. They never used a big car. There was a lot of sharp curves, right angle curves, on the north end run. I think that is the reason they used it. On those 300 cars, there wasn't any place to sit down. You had to stand up for six or eight hours. You had to stretch your arms out to work the controls. It was just a stand up job on those cars. There was a stool to sit on, but there wasn't any place to put your knees.

"Then after they broke you in, they put you on the little shuttle car up Broadway. Then you went from that to the Park Avenue run, then to Briscoe Run, and the last run you broke in on was the interurban to Marietta.

"The interurban was the hardest thing to learn because of the stops and turns. They also used train signals on the interurban the same as they did on the railroad. We didn't run on railroad tracks, but we used the same signals. For example, at 5:00 in the evening, they would put on extra sections. You had to put a flag up to indicate that there was another section coming behind you. At the switches, you would blow a signal, and he had to answer. The other car might be out of sight, and the fellow waiting at the switch might not be able to see him; this way, he would know he was coming. The Marietta run was a pretty lucrative run for the company.

"The Marietta run was the last one to go. When it shut down, all of the operators rode down; all of the operators rode on the last trip and got to run the last car. It was jam-packed.

"In the last, they operated streetcars and busses together. After the streetcars stopped, I drove the city lines busses until I retired.

"After the streetcars stopped, they dug pits in the old car barn to work on the busses. When they dug these pits, they found old mule shoes, singletrees, and a lot of things that was used for the mule-drawn streetcars in the beginning. They also said that they used to bury the old mules out behind the car barn (presently the Wood County Board of Education bus garage on 19th Street).

"When I first came to work, they still had the two-man cars. They used a conductor and a motorman on them. It was my privilege to conduct on the last two-man car that was in Parkersburg. The conductor just collected the tickets and fares, and loaded them (passengers) on and off at the back door. The motorman just drove. There was a pull cord, and the conductor would give him two signals to go, one signal to stop, and three to back up.

"It cost seven cents, a token, or a ticket to ride. Four tokens cost twenty-five cents. Then they had a red book they sold which was several tickets in a book. That was the cheapest way to buy them. People who rode the streetcars to work every day would buy the red book."

DIFFERENT CARS

"When I first started, they had a little streetcar that had a single truck in the middle of it, instead of a set of trucks on either end. It was strictly a shuttle car. It ran from O'Ames to the end of the line on Broadway. It was strictly for passengers living on Broadway. The passengers would get off the Viscose car and into the Broadway car. The only time they took that car off the Broadway run was when it had to be serviced. Two old fellows, Harry Eskey, and Tony Renner, was the operators on it. Harry wouldn't run anything else. They would put the extra board (substitute operators) on, on their days off. The extra board always liked to get that shuttle car run because you didn't have to worry about traffic on it. Car 621 was a car that everybody liked. It was a good car, and it had a whip-poor-will whistle on it.

"They had extra cars that they used as school cars, morning and evening. There was always about three trippers out of a morning to pick up school kids. When school was out, they'd line up at the high school and take them to Vienna, or wherever."

Streetcar hat used by Earl Booth.

SHIFTS

"They worked you first in, first out. If you were the first man in in the evening, you were the first out in the morning. Then, they had about seven or eight extra men. If a regular man would call off sick or something, they would call out an extra man.

"Then we had what we called an owl car that ran at night and took the men home after all the cars came in. Then, they had a pick up car in the morning. The 4:30 a.m. car went around north end, and a 4:30 a.m. car went over by the Viscose and picked up the operators to bring them to work. They also might pick up a few workers that had to go to work a little early in the morning. So, they picked up their own men to go to work or take them home after work in the evening."

EAT

"On the early cars, they ate on the car as they drove. Then later when they got the union, there would be an operator get on your car and go to the next switch and come back. That was all the time you had to eat. Sometimes you'd just get about fifteen minutes; operators would stop going up and leave their order. They'd have it ready on a tray for you when you came back down."

PROBLEMS

"The kids would grease the tracks for you on Halloween. They'd put transmission grease on the tracks. When they did that, you would just go like a sled. There at Vitrolite in Vienna, you would make a sharp left and go down a grade towards River Road. There was a sharp elbow turn, and you could alway expect that to be greased.

"One time Glen Backus came down 36th Street to turn onto Broad Street in a 300 type car on a Halloween night. He applied a little bit of air to slow down; it was a right angle turn, ninety degrees, and his wheels locked. He sanded. You had four sandboxes on your car right over the wheels. You opened valves underneath your sandbox, and that would let the sand out on your wheels. He sanded, and did everything. Finally, he threw it in emergency. He hit that ninety degree turn, and the door flew open. When you used the air brake, it took the air from your doors to close them. His stool flew out. They had bars to hold to as you walked up the stairs. He said he was holding onto that bar, and his feet was hanging out in the air. He didn't wreck; he was lucky.

"Another problem was with kids pulling your trolley rope. Those trolleys worked like a window blind. You would give a jerk, and that released the rope. The trolley is how you get your juice to run the streetcar. So, if someone would pull your trolley rope, the car would go completely black. When the kids would pull these trolley ropes on Halloween, it stopped your car. When this happened, the operator would have to get out and hit the trolley (until you found the wire). It would spark; then you could find the trolley and put your wheel back on.

"Then by the time you get back in the car, some kid would pull it again. So, one operator got the idea to put tacks through the trolley rope. He said when he would come in on Halloween night, his rope would be bloody, but I could never do someone that way."

ACCIDENTS

"One accident was up near the glass plant (Vienna) where the railroad crossing goes across the street. It was a snowy night, and they had quite a load on the streetcar, and the streetcar hit a steam engine (train). A steam pipe broke, and steam flew back through the car. I don't think anybody was killed, but they had some pretty severe injuries, bad burns.

"Another accident was when one of the interurban cars was coming down from Summit to Central, and a mule was on the track. I believe Tony Renner was operating the car, and a streetcar went over into a run, but I don't think anyone was killed.

"Then there was a store up near the Viscose, and a milkman pulled up and parked his truck too near the tracks. Just as the streetcar came, the milkman stepped out with those trays of milk; the streetcar hit him and killed him.

"Some operators like me had our share of accidents, but I wasn't the worst one of the bunch. One time up at Smith Crossing, I blew a long crossing whistle, and this fellow came along and never stopped. I had used most of my emergency air blowing the long crossing whistle. I applied the air, and it didn't stop as fast as it should. I hit him broadside and his car door blew open. I slid that car sideways down the track about the length of a street-

663 car was used to clean the tracks. Picture loaned by Nobel Schofield.

car before it would stop. I got out thinking the streetcar had just rolled over him and chewed him up. I couldn't find him, and I run back behind the front trucks. He was sitting right next to the wheels. I ran to a house to call an ambulance, and I called my dispatcher. I stayed there until the ambulance took him to the hospital. Then I went around the loop and back to Marietta, and there that guy stood. He was bandaged up; he had a bandage around his head, patches on his face, and one arm in a sling—but it wasn't broken. He said he had a few bangs and boasted that he would be all right. But I thought sure he would be killed.

"Another accident I had was over on South Parkersburg. A kid got out and threw a switch. There was a siding there with a coal car sitting in it. It was all grown over with grass. When you get a streetcar on grass or leaves, you've lost it. All of the motormen dreaded the fall of the year's leaves. They were worse than oil or grease. It was early Sunday morning, and I had about four people on the car. As soon as that car made that turn on that siding, I knew it was all over, and I threw it into emergency. It was one of those big cars, and I hit that thing for all it had. Glass shattered, and it just demolished the front of the streetcar. Just before it hit, I started back (through the car) to get away from the front end of the car. There was a little girl sitting right next to the aisle with her mother. When we hit, that little girl just flew right in my arms. If I hadn't been there to catch her, she would have gone into the front of that car. They blamed me because I should have seen the open switch. I think I served two or three days. If you had an accident, you served two, three, or four days without pay as penalty."

WEATHER

"Extreme changes from hot to cold weather caused problems. You had to get the line car out and either tighten up the trolley line or let the trolley line out. If the line got too tight, it would break. They would tighten up in cold weather, and in hot weather they would sag down. They would leave three or four feet of extra line at the switch pans where the trolley lines came together to handle the slack.

"I remember one big snow here and a streetcar was stuck. It sat at 7th and Market Streets for 31 days. I think once it thawed up to where the fire department could use the hose, they used water to melt the ice to get the car going."

SPEED

"There was hot spots near the substations. When you were close to those, you got more juice and the faster it would go. If you had a big load on, they wouldn't hardly pull Summit Hill. But coming down to Vienna from Summit, that thing would just fly. I would probably go 75 miles an hour. They would usually travel about 35 miles an hour.

"The streetcar line from Fairmont to Clarksburg, West Virginia was the fastest streetcar line in the United States. I have tried to keep up with them in a car and couldn't beat them on that line."

STOPS

"There were regular stops for the streetcars, usually at the corners in town. Then on the interurban line, you had Hobbies, Henderson, Dry Run, Middle Switch, and others. At night, the motorman would call out the stops. You would have to be familiar enough with the run to call out the stops. It was hard for passengers to see where the streetcar was after dark on the interurban."

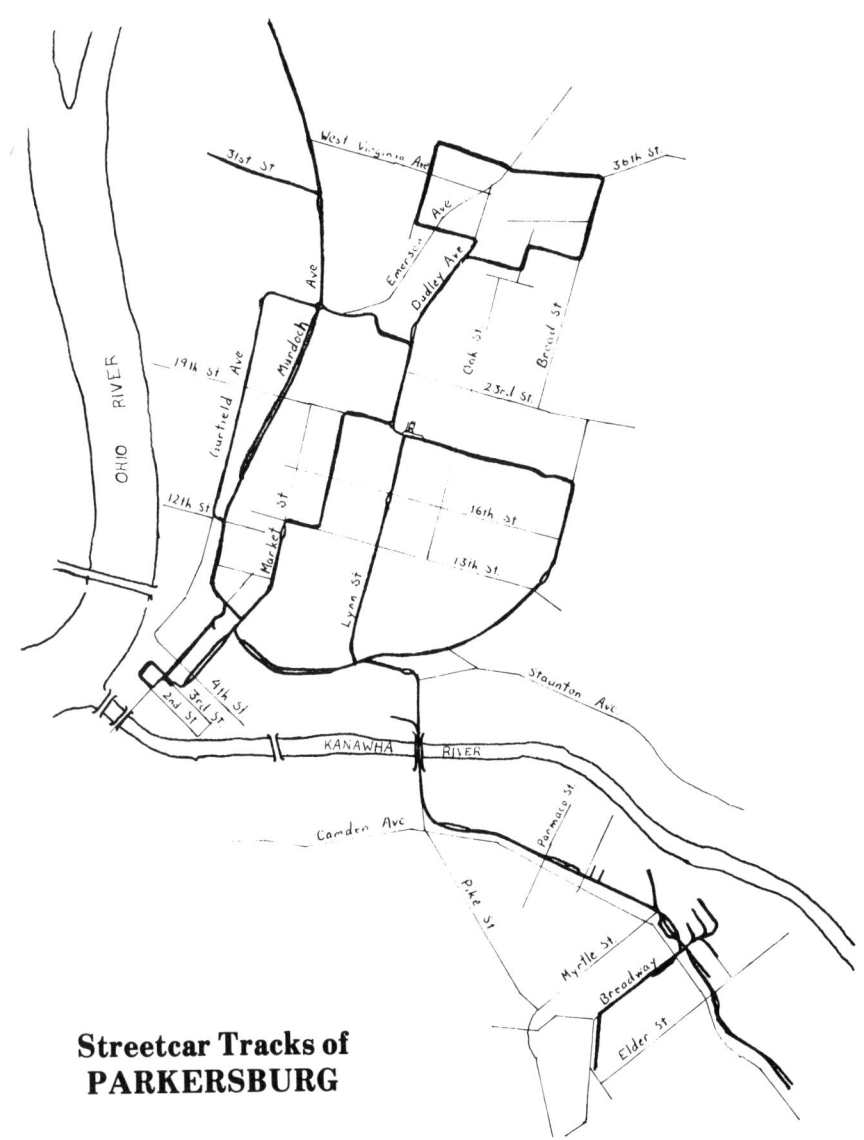

Streetcar Tracks of PARKERSBURG

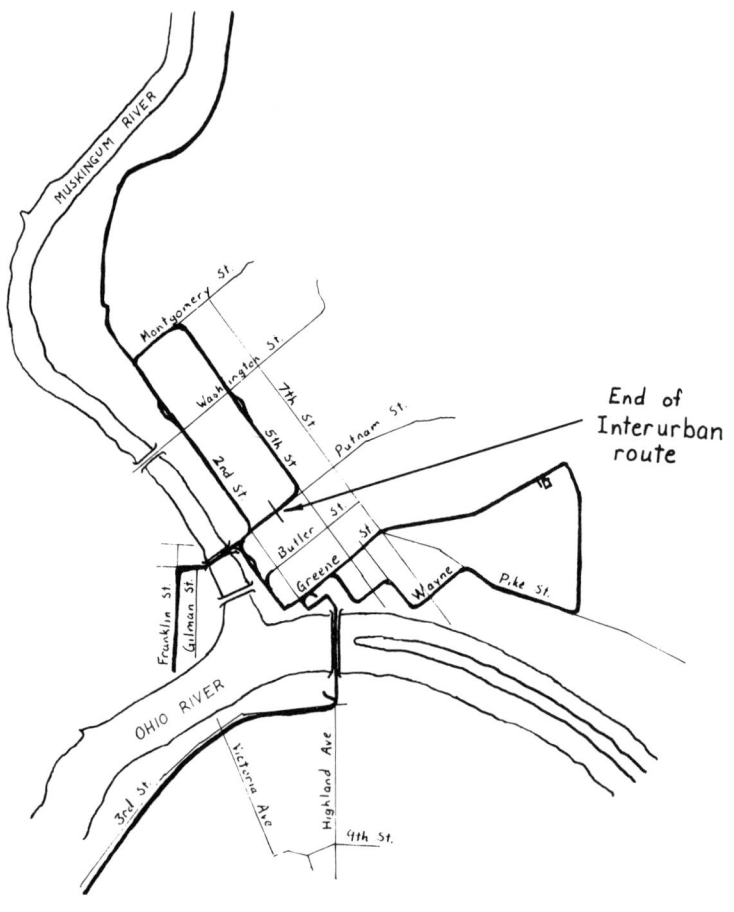

Streetcar Tracks of MARIETTA and WILLIAMSTOWN

Book II 191

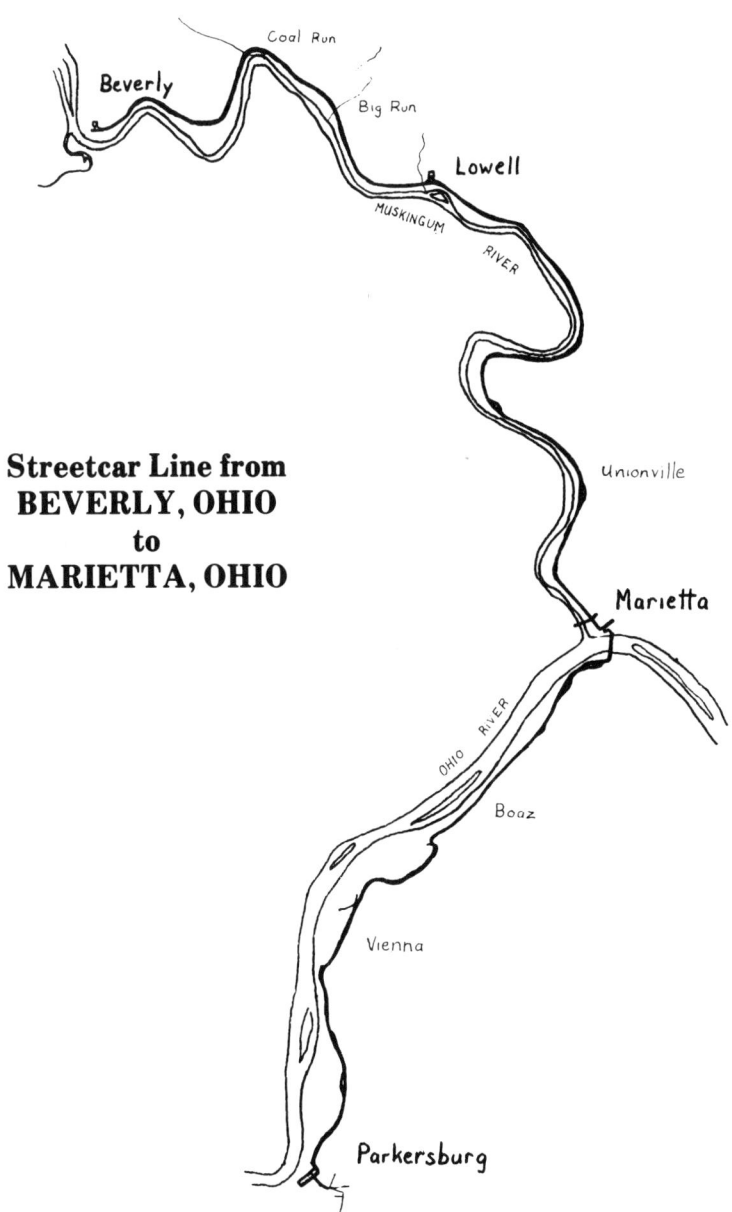

**Streetcar Line from
BEVERLY, OHIO
to
MARIETTA, OHIO**

Colonel Joseph Barker
by Janet Affolter and Kim Halley

As we walked into the home of Mrs. Margaret Barker Meredith, we were greeted with an instant feeling of warmth and comfort. In her home, traditions are revered and bits and pieces from the past are treasured.

Mrs. Meredith works at a monument shop and is nicknamed "Tombstone Annie," a strange name for such a petite and fragile lady. She is a very active person who keeps college students in her home and works in the shop in spite of a heart condition. Her warmth and kindness made us feel very much at home.

"Colonel Joseph Barker was my great-great grandfather. I am the last living member of the Barker family.

"The original part of this house that I live in was built about 1840 or 1850. My grandfather, Gage Barker, was the son of Colonel Joseph, and he bought this house and added the front addition which is four rooms and a hallway. It hasn't been changed since then.

"I have never lived anywhere else except for summer jobs, and when I was away at Lake Erie College. My father and mother lived here with his parents. It seemed to be the way they did in the Barker family.

"Then, my mother died; and my husband and I lived here with my father. Dad was a very easy going person so it seemed to work out well.

Mrs. Margaret Barker Meredith.

"Unfortunately, my grandfather was one of six boys and except for my grandfather, they all left this area. So, the original furniture of Colonel Barker left too. My grandfather stayed here to farm. There are two tables that they used for banquet tables here. My father had to buy one of them. There is also some silver pieces and dishes that were original family pieces.

"Colonel Barker was a man who believed in education. He had his children all tutored. I have a copy of his school bill for tutoring. My grandfather was sent to military school in New Hampshire. That was very unusual.

"Colonel Barker had ten children, four sons and six daughters. One son was drowned at the age of three in the Muskingum River.

"One of Colonel Joseph's daughters, Fanny Barker Gage, achieved prominence as a poet, author and lecturer. She traveled all over the country giving talks about temperance and women's rights.

Gage Barker house, occupied by Mrs. Meredith.

"She wrote a book of poems and two novels. One novel was the *Old Still House*. This one was about the Barker house. It was based on fact. Another daughter, Catherine, wrote a book when she was in her seventies. She remembered back when she was growing up. It tells in detail about her wedding. It must have been really beautiful. She wrote of the activities of the neighborhood. It is probably the only account of that time. Catherine also married a Barker, a different line of Barkers.

"The only thing left in the family records of Colonel Joseph's dealings with Harman Blennerhassett is a ledger. Parts of it are difficult to read, but one page still has a clear signature of Harman Blennerhassett. You can see where he bought quite a few small items for them from the stores in Marietta. They had him to pick up things at the store so they wouldn't have to run back and forth from the island.

"We had the contract for the mansion until my grandfather loaned it to a relative. We never got it back, so it might be anywhere. The Greene's house (Dr. F.P. Greene) in Williamstown is the replica of the Blennerhassett mansion.

"Colonel Barker was not a social person. He was purely business. He and the Devols did a lot of shipbuilding things together. They would take the boats down the Ohio then dismount and get back some other way. His recollections are at Marietta College. But, they tell nothing of the area. They are about his work on the river and that type of thing.

"Colonel Barker and my grandfather, Gage Barker, were both in the legislature. Colonel Joseph was commissioned as a colonel, not because of the Revolutionary War or any war, but because they had to have an Ohio militia to protect this country from the Indians. He was commissioned a captain and then a colonel. He was always known as colonel after that.

"Colonel Joseph came here in 1795. He received a grant of one hundred acres of land located at Wiseman's Bottom for his services in the Indian War. This land was located seven miles up the Muskingum River from the Ohio River and extended on either side of the river.

"He begun to clear the land and to set out some orchards and crops. He was compelled, as he put it, to hold his scalp on with one hand while he dug holes for trees with the other.

"On December 18th of that year, he moved the family to the farm which was to be his home for nearly fifty years.

"In addition to settling and developing his homestead, he built several homes for Marietta families.

"During the years of 1799 and 1800, he also built the splendid mansion for Harman Blennerhassett on the island just below Parkersburg, West Virginia. Several of the Marietta homes still stand today.

"In his shipbuilding business he built the *Brig Dominic* for Blennerhassett. In the same year he built the *Indiana*; and in 1803, he built the *Louisa.*

"In 1806, Dudley Woodridge placed an order for fifteen boats with Colonel Joseph. Burr, Woodridge, and Blennerhassett were interested in plans concerning the lower Mississippi Valley and Mexico. Thus, Joseph Barker became indirectly involved with the Burr and Blennerhassett scheme.

"The boats were to accommodate fifty men apiece, plus luggage. Ten of the boats were to be forty feet long, ten feet wide, and two and a half feet deep. Five were to be fifty feet long. They were to be pointed at both ends, so they would travel both upstream and down. They were to be built similar to skiffs.

"Blennerhassett called on the shipyard and informed Colonel Joseph that the boats were to be used for Burr's expedition. One of the boats was to be fitted out for the private use of Burr. It had partitions, fireplace, and glass windows. The boats were to be ready the tenth of December, and they were to be launched at night. Colonel Joseph was also urged to interest young men in the expedition. Blennerhassett promised to pay him three dollars for each man he could recruit.

"A week after Blennerhassett's visit, President Jefferson issued a proclamation warning against a conspiracy. On December 1, Governor Tiffin of Ohio received word at Chillicothe of suspicious movements of men and arms on the Ohio River. On December 5th, he and legislators met in a closed session and secretly passed a bill to au-

The top picture shows the window-facing in the new part of the Colonel Barker house. The picture to the right shows the window-facing in the old part of the house. Notice the difference in the craftsmanship.

thorize the seizure of the boats and supplies. Judge Return Jonathan Miegs and Major Joseph Buell were ordered to seize the boats.

"On the evening of December 9th, ten of the boats were seized at Marietta, Ohio. They had been launched and were on their way to Blennerhassett Island. Four unfinished and one finished boat were seized at the ship yard. The captured boats were used later to transport United States troops to St. Louis.

"Colonel Joseph Barker died September 21, 1843. It has been noted that on the following day, thirty-six carriages and many people on horseback and foot made up a funeral procession to his final resting place in the Putnam Cemetery in Devola, Ohio.

"There are six generations of the Barker family buried there in the Putnam Cemetery. There is a lot there waiting for me. My husband, Tom, and son, John, are buried there. I will be between them."

Exterior of the house.

Exterior of house.

The fine brick house which still stands on Colonel Joseph Barker's farm, with its recessed windows, its concealed chimneys, its Adam doorway, and its decorated interior woodwork, reveals Colonel Joseph's competence as a builder and architect. The original (front) part of the house was built around 1811. The new (back) addition to the house was added about 1860. The present owners of the house are Mr. and Mrs. Robert M. Ray, Jr.

Sitting room in the new part of the house.

Stairway in the old part.   **Dining room in the old part.**

The letters and documents reprinted in the story are originals from Colonel Joseph's files. The letters on the following pages are from two of Colonel Joseph's sons to each other. The next letter is from a son in the Civil War. The last letter is from a daughter, Fanny, who was well-known as a poet, author, and lecturer. All the letters and documents were loaned to us by Mrs. Meredith.

Amherst August 8th, 1796.

Dear Brother.

It is with the greatest pleasure I have an opportunity of writing to you for the first time, but I cannot accuse myself of negligence so much as if I had received a letter from you but now I hope you will write to me the first opportunity we received your letter with thankfullness but should much rather see you and I hope it will not be long before ever I do see you I have written one letter to Jerundana and another to William and I wish you would send it to them as soon as you have an opportunity. I have sent by your little boys (Joseph and Luther) some little thing to play with and Polly the little girl some things Ephraim wished to send a little book amongst the rest to remember him by I have nothing new to write

Joseph Barker. I remain your friend and Brother

Jon B Barker

Amherst August 8th, 1796

Dear Brother:

It is with the greatest pleasure I have an opportunity of writing to you for the first time, but I cannot accuse myself of negligence so much as if I had received a letter from you but now I hope you will write to me the first opportunity. We received your letters with thankfulness but should much rather see you and I hope it will not be long before we do see you. I have written one letter to Steven, Dana and another to William and I wish you would send it to them as soon as you have an opportunity. I have sent your little boys (Joseph and Luther) some little things to play with. Polly and Little Ephraim sends the little girl some things. Ephraim wishes to send a little book amongst the rest to remember him by. I have nothing new to write.

I remain your Friend and Brother,
Jon B. Barker

Camp of 34th Ohio Vet Vol Infy
near Harper Ferry Aug 7th /64

Dear Father,

As I have a little time to spare. I will write you a few lines this morning. Should have written you before but did not know where to direct in regards to the letters I wrote home to be forwarded you. No doubt you have heard before this all about our battle at Winchester and the different skirmishes we have been in. Have no time to give you a detailed account, as we expect to move every moment.

Our loss at Winchester now foots up 123 in Killed & Wounded. 11 Killed 112 wounded 17 missing. Capt Ford of Co E was killed Lt Montgomery, Haddow & Maj Palmer wounded 11 wounded & 2 missing in my Co. none killed Lt Geo Putnam was wounded & fell into the hands of the Enemy.

Our Regt has lost some 200 men since we came into Va. When our old men go out will have but a small squad left. I have made up my mind to leave the service if I can be mustered out. If not I will resign this fall. I am feeling pretty well, with the exception of being very tired and

and worn out from hard marching and loss of sleep. have marched almost every day since we left Parkersburg. fighting a good part of the time. I believe I have suffered more than I did on our Lynchburg raid. This is the fourth time we have passed through Harpers Ferry.

Have not heard a word from home since I left. would like to hear from Father. It is reported that Gen Grant came in on the train last evening. Gen Crook is Brevt Maj Gen & commands the forces in the field. The 6th & part of 19th Corps are here with Kanawha troop. The rebels are reported in a dozen different places Some at Hagerstown. Some at Cumberland Some crossing at Hancock. some reported in=trenching on old Antietam battle ground. I think but few rebel infantry have crossed into Pa. Only Cavalry. They are raiding through the country while Gen Early's forces gather the Crops in Shenandoah Valley.

Credily is calling for the letter. Direct 1st Brig 2d Inf 3 Div Crooks Comd

Your aff— Son
J. W. Barlow

Excuse poor writing. am sitting on ground under shelter tent.

Camp of the 36th Ohio Vet. Vol.
Infry., near Harpers Ferry, August 7th, '64

Dear Father:

As I have a little time to spare, I will write you a few lines this morning. Should have written you before but did not know where to direct so requested the letters I wrote home to be forwarded to you. No doubt you have heard before this all about our battle at Winchester and the different skirmishes we have been in. Have not time to give you a detailed account as we expect to move every moment. Our loss at Winchester now foots up 123 in killed and wounded. 11 killed, 112 wounded, 17 missing. Captain Ford of Co. E. was killed, Lt. Montgomery, Haddow and Maj. Palmer wounded. 11 wounded and 2 missing. In my Co. none killed. Lt. George Putnam was wounded and fell into the hands of the enemy.

Our Regt. has lost some 200 men since we came into virginia. When our old men go out will have but a small squad left. I have made up my mind to leave the service if I can be mustered out. If not, I will resign this fall. I am feeling pretty well, with the exception of being very tired and wore out from hard marching and loss of sleep. Have marched almost every day since we left Parkersburg, fighting a good part of the time. I believe I have suffered more than I did on our Lynchburg raid. This is the fourth time we have passed through Harpers Ferry.

Have not heard a word from home since I left. Would like to hear from Luther. It is reported that Gen. Grant came in on the train last evening. Gen. Crook is Brevet Maj. Gen. and commands the forces in the field. The 4th and part of the 19th Corps are here with Kanawha troops. The rebels are reported in a dozen different places some at Hagerstown, some at Cumberland, some crossing at Hancock, some reported in trenching on old Antietam battleground. I think but few (rebel) infantry have crossed into Pennsylvania, only Cavalry. They are raiding through the country while Gen. Early's forces gather the crops in Shenandoah Valley.

Orderly is calling for the letters. Direct 1st Brig 2nd Infry Div Crooks Comd.

Your aff son
J.G. Barker

Excuse poor writing am sitting on ground under shelter tent

Book II 205

Dr. Joseph Barker Esqr in A/C

1799
Mar. 2. To The Conductor Generalis 10/ $2.67
  Mentoria or ye Ladies Friend 6/ 1.
  3 Easy Steps 2/6 7/6 1.25 4.92
Apr. 8. To 2 Galo whiskey 4/6 12/ 21. 22.—
  Barrel 4/5 66/3 11. 4
May 14 To 15 yds. Linen 4/9 28/6 4.75
  6 yds. Ditto 9/ 2.84 18.63
  1 Blanket 40/6 1.75
June 21 To 1 Square 15/6 .58
  Set Cups & Saucers @ 1/6 4/6 .75
  3 pt. Bowl 1/ .17 3.25
  1 Cream pot 2/6 .41
  25 To ¼ lb. pepper 1/6 .25
  1 paper pins 3/ .50
  1 yd. India Chintz @ 10/6 31/6 5.25
  3 pr. Nankeen
  deld Isaac Barker on 6.20.
  A sum paid for J. Barker 31/- 5.14 11.58
  .67
  27 To 4 lb. 2 oz. Butter @ 1/ 4/1 1.86
  1 Tin pail 5/6 .92 3.25
  1 Tin pan 1/ .17
  1 Quire Letter paper 6/ 1.
  28 To 1 Gal. whiskey 1/6 .25
  1 qt. Delf mug 4/3 .71
July 2 To 1 Delf Bowl 6/ 7/6 1.25
  3 To 2 Gals. whiskey 6/ 1. 6.38
  ½ lb. Bok Tea 1/ 4/ .67
  5 lb. Butter @ 1/2 4/ .53
  4 To 2 lb. Roll Brimst @ 1/ 2/ .33½
  ¼ lb. Glaub Salts 4/ 2/ 1.37½
  ½ oz. Ginger
  ½ lb. 6 Salt
  1 2 l. Cognac Brandy 9/ 15/ .50
  5 To 2 Doz. Needles
  1 6 Salt. Line
  6 To 1 lb. raisins
  8 To 1 2t. whiskey by Self
  9 To 21 lb. salt pork
  3 plates
  1 Set Knives & Forks
  ½ lb. Nistard by Selby

Errors Excepted
Septr 23. 1799
Harn Blennerhassett

A bill to Colonel Joseph owed by **Harman Blennerhassett**. Notice the original Blennerhassett signature inserted.

Letter, written about 1859, from Frances Dana Gage ("Aunt Fanny"), daughter of Joseph Barker, to her brother-in-law Francis Barker of McConnelsville, Ohio, and later of Iowa.

St Louis Dec 1st

Brother Francis,
    Last Thursday which should have been the time for my weekly letter, I was too sick to write — confined by a terrible cold, which produced inflammation, or nearly that of the lungs its — Monday previous my Good House Keeper was called away by a sick sister & I was trying to do alone. I got help however for a few days, & am now trying to get along so till Eliza returns. We have heard that Mary E. Gage is not well at Yellow Springs — (I friend wrote to James she was not) tho' she asserts that she is — And I think we shall one or both of us go on before long, & see to things there. I don't half like the idea of her trying to study & keep house. It compels her to be too much out of society & she is one that needs a frolic now & then. If the sisters have resolved to go home before cold weather, they can accompany us. Tho' I hope they will not. so decide decide —
Or if they will spend a month with me. Chas. I think will go on in Jan —
I wish one of them would come & stay with me. if both to Monroe will spare both.

or rather come & stay with the family, & while I let me go—to work for humanity. But it is so lonely here I dare not ask it tho I would pay good wages.
Sarah would instantly return—if asked—But I know that Sarah's health, happiness, & mentality depends upon her being kept out from home for a time. We have not decided whether we can both go to Ohio or not But I am urging Mr Goye to go this once with me, & see our children. & as he wants to buy potters in Cincinati or Pittsburgh May be we can make it go—So the sisters can go now—or in January—or in the spring—or Charlotte can go & leave S— to spend the winter with me if she can not be content to remain. But I do hope neither will think of returning before spring—and I dont think you have any right to both all winter—So you choose first & give me the other. for if I sit here all alone,—I shall go to writing novels or something, sure as the world.
Friends all well when heard from—
            Yours Truly
              Sister Fanny

St. Louis December 1st

Brother Francis:

Last Thursday which should have been the time for my weekly letter, I was too sick to write - confined by a terrible cold, which produced inflammation, or nearly that of the bowels - Monday previous my good housekeeper was called away by a sick sister and I was trying to do alone. I got help however for a few days and am now trying to get along till Elisa returns. We have heard that Mary E. Gage is not well at Yellow Springs - a friend and father and I think we shall one or both of us go on before long and see to things there - I don't half like the idea of her trying to study and keep house. It compels her to be too much out of society and she is one that needs a frolic now and then. If the sisters have resolved to go home before cold weather, they can accompany us. Tho' I hope they will not. So decide - or if they will spend a month with me. Charles I think will go on in Jan.--I wish one of them would come and stay with me - if Catherine won't spare both - or rather come and stay with the family a while, and let me go to work for humanity. But it is so lonely here I dare not ask it tho' I would pay good wages.

Sarah would instantly return if asked - But I know that Sarah's health, happiness, and mentality - depends upon her being kept out from home for a time. We have not decided whether we can both go to Ohio or not. But I am urging Mr. Gage to go this once with me, and see our children, and as he wants to buy (patterns?) in Cincinnati and Pittsburgh. Maybe we can make it go - So the sisters can go now - or in January - or in the spring - or Charlotte can go and have 8 to spend the winter with me if she cannot be content to remain - But I do hope neither will think of returning before spring--and I don't think you have any right to both all winter - So you choose first and give me the other, for if I sit here all alone, - I shall go to writing novels or something, as sure as the world. Friends all well when heard from -

In the name and by the authority of the State of Ohio.

RETURN JONATHAN MEIGS, Governor and commander in chief of the said state,

To Mr. Joseph Barker — — — — Greeting:

It being certified to me that you are duly elected lieutenant of the second company in the second battalion, first regiment, first brigade, and third division of militia in this state. Now know you, That by virtue of the powers vested in me by the constitution and laws of said state; and reposing special trust and confidence in your courage, activity, fidelity and good conduct, I do by these presents, commission you as Lieutenant of said Company, hereby authorising and requiring you to discharge all, and singular, the duties and services appertaining to your said office, agreeably to law, and such instructions as you shall from time to time, receive from your superior officers.

In Testimony Whereof, I have hereunto set my name, and caused the great seal of the State of Ohio to be affixed at ZANESVILLE, the fourth day of January — in the year of our Lord one thousand eight hundred and eleven and in the thirty-fifth year of the independence of the United States of America.

By his Excellency's command,

Jn. Winn Secretary of State

Return Jonathan Meigs

Terrapin Park

by Ann Bailey and Kellie Grimm

A source of entertainment in early Parkersburg, West Virginia, for almost two decades was Terrapin Park. It was considered the best amusement park in the state. In its day, the park boasted not only the famous Casino but a large artificial lake, a picnic area, a playground and several carnival rides.

Although the actual construction date is still a controversy,

Casino at Terrapin Park — Loaned by Fred Mayer.

most people agree that it was built just before 1900. The park was destroyed by a fire around the end of the first World War (1917). With its burning went many happy memories. Some of these memories have been recaptured with the help of Mr. Willard Jackson and Mrs. Helen White.

Today, when Terrapin Park is mentioned, most of us think of an old, overgrown, wooded area that provides a short cut home from school. But as we learned, it is more than that. It is a part of our city's history that should not be forgotton.

The park proved profitable not only to its owners but to area businesses as well. Among these were the streetcar lines. There were two main lines, the outer loop and the inner loop ("Pottery Junction"), now the Murdoch Avenue and Emerson Avenue junction. Both took their passengers directly to the gate at Terrapin for a nickel. The park was located between Dudley Avenue and Bull Creek Road (now Emerson Avenue).

Each person paid admission upon entering the park. An additional fee was charged for the rides and shows. Mr. Jackson describes the entrance to the park.

"One would enter the park at its southeast corner through an attractive, large wooden gate. As one entered, there was a merry-go-round that was enclosed for all-weather use on the left and a large roller coaster on the right. Wooden booths lined the midway back to the casino with all kinds of carnival gimmicks. Towards the lake, between the roller coaster and the casino, was a large one story frame pavilion that contained an indoor roller skating rink."

Located in the southern, central portion of the park was the famed casino. The massive three story building was built by Charles Shattuck shortly before 1900. Beautiful verandas surrounded the structure with two towers in its southeast and southwest corners. Some of the casino's attractions included a dance hall, theatre, pool room, and an auditorium.

The auditorium featured such guests as Maude Adams and W.C. Fields. It seated 1,500 persons but could be enlarged to accommodate as many as 2,000 people. This was accomplished by rolling up the large doors, which served as walls, thus making use of the verandas. Park benches were brought inside to provide extra seating.

The stage was known to have the finest and most expensive

Dazy Dazier Dip Roller Coaster at Terrapin Park.

array of scenery in the city. Downtown movie houses often borrowed some of the equipment from the auditorium.

Another major feature of the park was the "Dazy Dazier Dip Roller Coaster." Unlike the roller coasters of today, this one was made of wood. Built by Henry L. Brenig, the roller coaster was one of the most popular and exciting rides. It cost a dime for adults to ride and a nickel for children. Mr. Brenig was also responsible for the construction of the merry-go-round, skating rink, and dance hall.

At the northern end of the park was the lake. In the summer, skiffs could be rented for boating; and in the winter months, it was used for ice skating. After the fire, the lake was drained because it was considered dangerous. Now all that is left is a small stream.

Paul and Jack Crane took over the park in 1916 until September of 1917 when it burned. During the last months of its existence, the park began to take on a neglected look and was steadily going downhill. It is said that the management soon began to slacken in the enforcement of good conduct, and a certain amount of rowdyism was permitted. Mrs. White puts it this way:

"It was an awful blow to the people, but it had really passed its peak at the time that it burned. Unfortunately, the insurance on the park had lapsed just eight days prior to the fire. As a result, there were not sufficient funds to rebuild the park.

The exact cause of the fire still remains a mystery. Many rumors were circulated. One of the more popular speculations was that it was started by a religious fanatic who believed that people had no right to enjoy themselves when their sons were being killed in the war. As Mrs. White said, "... it isn't really important how it burned. The thing is that it was burned, and it was burned in anger."

"Although it was near midnight, there were many witnesses to the spectacular fire. It seems that it started somewhere underneath the stage and slowly made its way to the pillars, enveloping them in flames one by one. The American flag flew at the top of the casino, and soon the flames licked all around it. There was enough wind, breeze and heat from the fire to keep the flag waving. The sight of the proudly flying flag surrounded by hungry flames was an awesome one. Miraculously, the flag did not catch on fire until the entire building collapsed. Many of the spectators took this to be an omen that the United States would win the war, and that everything would work out for the best."

Today, without the aid of pictures and memories of those who lived in Parkersburg during the Terrapin Park era, one would find it hard to believe that such a fabulous funland ever existed. Part of the former park grounds now have medical offices on them, and another part has the YWCA on it. The remaining portion is covered by trees and overgrown weeds and bushes.

Had Terrapin Park not burned, it probably would have continued to deteriorate. More than likely, it would have been torn down so that it would not have stood in the path of progress.

In a remote way, the burning of Terrapin Park seems to represent the end of a totally different life-style; for a nickel, one could ride to one of the most beautiful parks in West Virginia, and spend a few more nickels on rides and games. Then for another nickel, one could ride home. The burning of Terrapin Park was one of the many changes which resulted in the end of an era.

Mr. Helmick

by Bill Snider and Mike Thronin

"My father was Abraham B., or Benjamin, Helmick. His family was from Pendleton County. His first wife was Katherine Mullenax. After they were married, they moved into Tucker County, where he bought a farm. Well, he didn't buy a farm, he bought a patch of woods. There was no place to build a house. I've heard him tell more than once they had to cut trees down and roll the logs back and make room to build the house. They built a log house. Now he and his first wife lived in there until she passed away.

"After she died, then he married Prodence Weir from Randolph County. They lived in the same house for a while; then as he cleared more land and as he got a little more prosperous, he built a nicer house, made of not logs but of boards. He and his second wife lived there until she passed away. When she died, he married my mother, Ida Emma Corina Knapp. They lived in the new house. He still continued to clear more land, and he raised stock and farmed. He was a hard worker.

"We all had to work as soon as we got able to pick up chips off the wood yard and carry a pail of water or to drive the chickens out of the yard or out of the garden when they got in. Any little thing like that, we had to start working.

"I remember we had flowers all around our yard. We never spaded up the flower beds in the spring; we just went out in the chip yard and raked back the chips and got fresh dirt. We had to have all the chips out of the dirt. My, did I dread that job! Fill those flower beds all the way around you know, for more flowers that year.

"One morning after my father and mother were married, they woke up about two in the morning and the house was on fire. Everybody got out of the house alive, but all the furniture they got out was one rocking chair and a sewing machine. They didn't have any insurance; that was before the days when everybody had insurance for everything.

"They had to move back in the log house until he could build another house, which was the nicest house because he was more prosperous and was more able to build. So that way, he had three wives and he built each one of them a new house, but they all lived in the log house.

"Well, I was the fourteenth child in a family of seventeen. It was a large family by him being married three times. My father used to tease my mother and say he took a nap and when he woke up it was too late. Her last name was Knapp.

"My mother's parents moved from Barbour County into Tucker County, and they lived upon what was called Haddocks Creek. I've gone with her on the back of a horse and rode the crupper strap. That's the strap that runs from the saddle back around under the horse's tail so the saddle won't shove forward on the horse's shoulder and rub it sore when you are going down a hill. If you want a nice ride, ride that for nine miles. Now, nine miles is 15 minutes more or less, but in those days nine miles was almost half a day if not a full day. The roads were either muddy or dusty or snowy, and it was always rocky in spots. I've gone many times with her on horseback. I don't know why she didn't take the buggy. I've wondered about it many times since I've grown up. Maybe she thought, due to the conditions of the roads, it was easier to ride horseback.

"We had a dug a well in our yard. They dug down to solid rock before they struck water. Above that was dirt and some of the boards finally got rotten. Some of the dirt would fall and some of the surface water would get in, so we never used that only to fill the old Home Comfort Range reservoir.

"Always those old Home Comfort Ranges and some of the other ranges had a reservoir. You filled that with water; then that was hooked up to the firebox that heated your water. So, when you wanted hot water for anything, why you went over to the reservoir and dipped it out. We used that for washing dishes. But, for cooking and drinking water, we carried that from down under the hill. At the spring where it came out under the hill, it was wonderful, fine water! I've wished many times I could go back there and sit on the edge of the trough, put my glass under the spout, and catch myself a good fresh drink of water that didn't have chlorine in it. It was fresh pure water right out of the hill.

"The people who lived in our community (Sugarlands) were as I have often said, 'the salt of the earth.' They were good people. Only one man ever went to jail and that was a fellow who liked his whiskey. That was in the days of the old saloon. That fellow, when he went to town, couldn't stay away from that saloon. His horse would sometimes get so doggoned skinny that he was ashamed to take him into town. Also, he was afraid the humane society might get after him for not treating his animals any better. He once tied his horse across the river from Thomas, West Virginia, walked into town and got to drinking. He had actually gone to town for the doctor for his wife who was confined. She had sent him for the doctor. Well, the doctor wasn't in at the time. So, what was wrong with him going to the saloon and having a ten cent drink while the doctor came in? As I say, one called for another and another, and he forgot what he went for. He got drunk. They knew his horse was over across the river somewhere, so they put him in jail and went and hunted up his horse and fed it and took care of it. When he got home, the baby was three days old. It happened that his brother came up to visit him that weekend. He found out what was going on and went for a neighbor who was a midwife, and she came over and took care of her. So they got along all right. They (officers) didn't know what was going on at home.

"Well anyhow, as the saying goes, those were the good old days. They had people very much like today. There were good people and there were bad. We had none of this street rioting, striking and carrying on like that. In our neighborhood everybody was good. Not everybody went to church, but they believed in it. They were just good people who worked hard.

"They called our section Sugarlands because of the sugar timber up there. Different people had sugar orchards. You tapped the trees about this time of the year (spring). They would get elder bushes and push the pith out and that would be the spouts. They would whittle the ends off to fit in the hole in the tree that they drilled with an auger. Then they made their troughs, sugar troughs, out of wood. They couldn't make it too big. It had to be so they could handle it, lift that trough up and pour it into the buckets.

"Then they had to boil it. At that time they just put it into an open kettle. But then they had what they called evaporators. That's a pan, maybe a foot deep and, depending on how big your sugar orchard was, maybe six to ten feet long. The fire was under it burning. It had little gates in there so it had to circulate around a certain way. You poured the water in one end; as it circulated through the trough at a certain speed, it came out maple syrup at the other end."

SNOWS

"They got big. I'll tell you, when it would snow up there in the fall it didn't leave until spring. It stayed all winter. It would fill in the rail fences and we had to shovel so the horses could get through. Then finally in the spring when it began to thaw, we were afraid to travel the road because a horse might break through that snow and break a leg. We had that hazard. Sometimes the snow was higher than the road bed. When it would come to one of those bad snows, the whole community would turn out with their snow shovels and open the road in case of sickness so the doctor could come.

"When it was winter time, we didn't always have church or Sunday school. It would be so cold and the roads would be so drifted, we could hardly get there."

SCHOOL

"We never wondered if we were going to school because when we got old enough, we were going come rain or shine or snowdrifts or what have you. We were all going to school.

"The school was a regular board one. I remember the roof leaked and the floor got wet, and it swelled up and it humped in the middle. I know the middle boards where it was humped was six inches higher than the others. It was a one room school with 53 in the enrollment. They had from the ABC class to the eighth grade. You could just know there would be a class on the floor reciting at all times. We had a recitation bench up front in the school.

"There was sort of a platform with about a 6 or 8 inch raise. That is where the teacher was, and that is where you went up to write on the blackboard. The blackboard was just boards painted black. There was no slate, just the boards; and when that wore off, you just painted them again. I suppose they had a certain kind of paint they used.

"There was just one teacher for all of them. They were real strict, and it was not unusual to see some switches standing in the corner.

"We had one boy that was never considered quite normal. Oh, he went to school and he did learn some, but he was just not normal. Every time I'd look at him, he was rubbing his fist under his nose. That meant at noon when we had a recess, we'd have a fight. He was three years older than me, but I was bigger then him. I was always a pretty good size for my age, and I could always get the best of him. What it amounted to was just a wrestle. I'd throw him down and hold him until he'd say he'd be good. I would never really hit him or anything because I felt sorry for him. My brother told me that he'd never let me alone until I mauled him. So finally one day during the summer after we had been swimming, he picked a quarrel and I got him down and mauled him real good. He never bothered me after that.

"The schoolhouse burned down one night. We never knew why. It was when school was not in session. Maybe they had to burn it down to get some of the students out who would have never got out otherwise. Then too, we had one man in particular who wanted the schoolhouse up closer to where he lived. Maybe he thought that was the one way to do it. It might have been an arson job too, we just never knew. But anyhow they bought an acre of ground off my father's farm to build a new schoolhouse. So that's where I went to school then. It was a one room school too. The wind blew so hard up there that they had to put what you call 'dead men' out there. That is, they dug holes in the ground and made cement and anchored it with cables to those 'dead men' on both sides of the schoolhouse. This kept the schoolhouse from blowing crooked. I was almost like the boy who when the teacher asked him why he was late said that every time he took a step he slid back two. So when she asked how I got to school, I said that I turned around and started toward home and slid back two and got to the schoolhouse. It was just about that hard to get to school sometimes.

"That one room school had some advantages. When you started in the ABC class, you also heard the people reciting in the Primer and in the Second Reader and the Third Reader all the way to the 8th grade. By the time you got up there, you about already knew part of the work just from hearing it all those years.

"Sometimes my father would hook the team of horses up to the bobsled and take us to school. It was a treat for us to get to ride in that bobsled. I don't know of anyone else in the neighborhood that ever took anyone in a sled to school. But my father was that kind of father. He was kind and good to us, but didn't spoil us. I remember one

Dewey Helmick

time we were going to school. We had a bad snow and we missed the road and got over the edge; the sled upset and threw all of us out but one of my brothers and the school teacher. They were under the sled in the snow, and we had to get them out of there real quick before they suffocated. I don't know, maybe they weren't in a hurry to get out. I think my brother liked that teacher pretty well. She was young and about his age, and he wasn't married and she wasn't either. Sometimes my dad would come to school with the sled and surprise us. It was just a little extra feature.

"In the wintertime we didn't always have church or Sunday school because it would be so cold and the roads would be so drifted that we could hardly get there. But when there was Sunday school, we didn't ask if we were going because we were going for sure. And you didn't play off sick because by the time my mother cooked us some vervain tea or some boneset tea, you had to really be sick or you would confess that you was a well person. The treatment was worse than the ailment. I'll tell you that vervain tea would pucker you up till you could hardly talk. And the boneset, you couldn't put enough sugar in it or take the bitterness out.

"My mother knew all the herbs. We would gather in the herbs during the summer and fall. Then in the wintertime, they would go out and peel off the rough bark of the wild cherry tree and get the inner bark. We cooked that with mullen leaves and made a real strong tea; and then we would put rendered hemp in there and cook her down to a syrup, and that was our cough syrup. I've made cough syrup more than once. It tastes pretty good; I didn't mind getting a cough you know 'cause it tasted pretty good. It wasn't the most effective cough remedy, but it helped. It was better than nothing."

LOG ROLLING

"They'd have log rollings; people would clear their land and dig out the little trees and stumps. They burned up thousands of cubic feet of mighty good lumber in logs that would be worth a fortune now, but then it was sort of worthless. Then there was no market for it, and the only thing you could do was use it for firewood, and everybody had more firewood than they knew what to do with. So we'd have log rollings. Log rollings was where you went and rolled all those logs up into heaps; then when they dried out good, why, you'd burn them. You couldn't keep it till it amounted to anything 'cause by that time it would rot.

"Those logs were pretty big around; some of them you had to roll because you couldn't get enough men to carry them. They'd have what you call 'handspikers.' Now a handspiker is a pole about six feet long, preferably made from hickory. Someone gets a hold of one end and someone the other; and you get about six guys under a big boy and carry that log off to where you want it. There you'd have a couple of smaller logs on which you roll it up onto the pile.

"I remember there was a man as big as an ox, and we were at a log rolling. I was then about eighteen, and I guess they must have thought we were the strongest, and they got each of us on the end of a handspike, the heavy end of the log you know. He wasn't about to buckle his knees and I wasn't either, so we come up with it. When we raised it up, the others shoved their poles under it, and we took off and carried it over to where they were stacking them up. After they dried out, we burned them.

"One time we had a log heap at home that we never got around to burning. At Easter, my brother and I would snitch eggs a little ahead of time, a couple each day. Then at Easter, we'd come in with a lot of eggs.

"My brother and I were laying eggs aside, oh, we didn't start so early that they'd spoil, but we wanted to make sure that they weren't taken off to the market and sold.

"Well, my brother got a pan at home; it was a bread pan. He got water in it and put in a half dozen eggs and set it on the log heap in a place so that when we set it on fire, the water would boil and cook our eggs. But when they got cooked, it was so hot we couldn't get the eggs. My mother, she wondered whatever happened to that pan. I tell you, my brother never had to tell me not to say anything, and I didn't have to tell him not to. We knew what would happen if we did. He was the one that snitched the pan. But I was a party to it. Lots of funny things happened."

CIVIL WAR

"When my father was a young man over in Pendleton County, he had several brothers; their father went off and joined the Confederate Army. They treated him real well. I think the reason for that was because he had these sons at home, and they wanted them to join too. If he went back saying how nice and wonderful it was in the army, they'd want to join too, which they did. So my father and his brothers and his father were in the Confederate Army. After about two years of that, my father was home on furlough, and was in the field working some distance from the house. He had left his jacket with his furlough papers at the house. A couple of Confederate soldiers came along and asked him, 'What are you doin here?' And he said, 'Well I'm on furlough.' They said 'Well, where are your papers?' And he said, 'They're down to the house in my jacket; you go down with me and I'll show them to you, or you can wait here and I'll go get them.' Well there was danger either way. If they went down, there might be someone waiting to bump them off with a rifle as they come. Or if they waited, he might not return. So they didn't take any chances on it; they just took him prisoner. He was put in Liddy Prison in Richmond, Virginia; that was really a prison for Union soldiers, but they just put him in there temporarily until they found out whether or not he was on furlough.

"While he was in there those few days, it didn't take those Union soldiers very long to recognize that he was a Confederate by his uniform, and they began to talk to him. They sort of brainwashed him, told him he was fighting for the wrong side. He resolved that when he got out, he would desert. When he got back to his company, he confided to his brother-in-law and he said, 'When you go, I'll go too.' He said, 'No, you can't go with me, you can go on your own, but you can't go with me.' Now you know what it means when anyone deserts, it means court-martial. That, of course, meant death. They didn't hem-haw around about it. There weren't several trials, and they didn't carry it all the way up to the Supreme Court. They just took care of you before the firing squad. So my father said, 'I don't want to be responsible for you; I'll be responsible for me; you be responsible for yourself. Now you go or you come, but you can't go with me.' He said he had several chances to desert, but he just couldn't shake that brother-in-law, because he kept an eye on him all the time. But one day they were going through this corn field, he was with his brother-in-law, and they were hunting for roasting ears. He was pretending to be opening them up and looking for good ones while all the time he was working away from them. When he got out of sight and he hoped out of hearing, he took off, and he heard something behind him. Now he looked around and there was that brother-in-law. My father said, 'Now you go back,' and they argued there until it was too late for either one of them to go back, because they'd wonder where they'd been and they'd be in trouble. They went on and hid around during the day and traveled at night. Once, in crossing the Shenandoah Valley, they came out into open fields and could look down into the lower part of the valley, and they saw what they thought to be a river. Well, they didn't want to tackle that river in the dark because they didn't know how deep it was or where the ford was. There weren't any bridges like there are now, so they decided to camp out. They spread out their blankets right out in that open field and Father said he couldn't rest, much less sleep. He couldn't sleep there because he might wake up right in sight of the wrong people. So he said to his brother-in-law, 'I'm going to cross that river if it's possible.' My father could swim and he said, 'I'm going to try it.' When they actually got down to it, it was fog settled in the valley and was no river at all.

"Another experience, this was early in the morning, and they were watching ahead and behind on all sides. They had to eat once in a while, and they came along to this house that wasn't very far from the road. So they went over and they didn't know what kind of reception they'd get because they had on Confederate outfits, or whether the people that lived there were Union or Confederate sympathizers. It happened that the woman came to the door was on their side or at least a Confederate sympathizer. They said, 'We're hungry, and we need something to eat. And we've gotten away from our outfit, which way would be most likely for us to run into them?' Well, there was a fork in the road on ahead a little bit, and she told them to take a certain fork. So when they got something to eat they went, didn't stay and eat it, and went up the fork she said until they were out of sight of the house. Then, they cut over to the other. Now they weren't wanting to meet anybody, especially their own people. Anyhow, when they got back in their neighborhood, he met this old lady who they called Aunt Becky. Now he was homesick and worried and concerned that he had left and deserted the Army. He was so happy to see someone he knew, and he knew he could trust her. He just ran up to her and threw his arms around her and said, 'Oh my, Aunt Becky, I'm so glad to see you!' And she said, 'Abe, what in the world are you doing here?' 'Well,' he said, 'Aunt Becky, I've deserted.' 'Oh,' she said, 'My God, Abe, the Calvary's just around the corner.' He jumped into the bushes and, he didn't have time to go very far or hide himself very good. He thought his heart was beating loud enough for them to hear it when they went past. Afterwards, he managed to get on in home and said to his wife, 'Give me some blankets, I'll have to sleep out tonight.' And she did. It just happened that the midwife came to the door and said, 'Well, I've got a notion to hit you over the head with something; you've got a son here.' And their oldest child had been born. He didn't take any chances going in to see the new child; he took to the woods. That night he ventured in to get a glimpse of his son, got to hold him a little bit, and then went back to the woods. That went on for a week or ten days. Finally, he came in and told his wife he didn't like the idea of hiding around and taking the risk of getting caught at any time. So he told her he was going to join the Union Army. He finished out the remaining two years of the war on the Union side and was involved in several skirmishes along the B and O Railroad toward Washington, D.C. At the Battle of Gettysburg, he was wounded in the left shoulder. He said he wasn't sure just when that bullet hit him; he was bent over loading his gun. When he went to raise that arm, it had just sort of numbed it. He didn't know whether or not it had hit just then or a little previous to that, but it hadn't hit when he bent over to load his gun. Pretty soon, of course, the pain set in and he knew he had been hit. When he first went into battle, he said that he felt a certain amount of fear; but as soon as that first shot was fired, all fear left him, and he wasn't afraid of nothing."

Borland Springs Hotel
by Mike Bostaph and Fred Mayer

If one were to drive about eighteen miles east on Route Fifty from Parkersburg, turn up the gravel road marked Borland Springs and continue about three more miles, one would find it very difficult to imagine that at one time a large hotel and mineral springs resort was located there.

Today, all one is able to find are the foundations to the once beautiful white buildings that graced the countryside. Trees and brush now cover the once manicured lawns, and the springs are not more than water holes. One can't help but find oneself thinking about the beauty and splendor of yesterday.

We talked with Mr. Charles Leavitt, whose father was the last owner of the hotel, about his memories of the resort.

"Borland Hotel was built by a Mr. Grimm in 1910. In about two or three years, he added a second addition to it. He operated the hotel until about 1926-1927. At that time several businessmen, Dr. Hartman, Dr. Robinson, Mr. Stork, and Mr. Gibbons, bought it from Mr. Grimm for $38,000.00. The businessmen were going to sell shares of stock to pay for it.

"The corporation didn't sell enough stock and still needed about $10,000.00. Dr. Robinson came to the funeral home and talked to my dad, Mr. Carr Thomas Leavitt, and he paid the note off. He borrowed the money from his brother-in-law to pay the note off.

"The corporation was supposed to keep the interest paid, the property in repair, fire insurance, and keep a caretaker at the hotel. They didn't do any of these things, and the building started running down with the roof leaking. My dad contacted the stockholders and informed them that he was going to sell the property. They didn't want it, and Mr. Leavitt brought suit against the stockholders, and it was sold at the courthouse. Mr. Leavitt was the only person to bid, and he bid $5,000.00 and got the property.

"The Leavitts re-opened the hotel and ran it from 1933-1937. At that time they closed it, but re-opened it for a season in 1941. They re-roofed the springhouse and spent large sums of money on road repair between the hotel and Route Fifty. It was never a paying venture, so the hotel was closed permanently in 1941. With the coming of the automobile, people started traveling more and were going greater distances for their vacations. After closing the hotel, Mr. Leavitt hired a man to live in the building to care for it. He later started drinking, and Mr. Leavitt disapproved of the drinking and moved him out. This was

Borland Springs Hotel — Picture loaned by Charles Leavitt.

Dining Room at Borland Springs Hotel—Picture loaned by Charles Leavitt.

Spring House at Borland Springs Hotel—Picture loaned by Charles Leavitt.

late in the winter; by spring, vandals had wrecked the building. They had torn up the furniture, broken the windows out, and stolen the linen and silverware.

"The building was then used for raising broiler chickens. The chicken business became unfeasible, and the buildings were further destroyed by vandals.

"Finally, it caught fire and burned early one morning in 1951 or 1952. The hotel contained sixty-two rooms. The spa was known for its mineral waters, making it one of the favorite vacation spots and health spas in the country.

"In its heyday, it was reproduced on post cards, where it was pictured as a three-story white frame structure nestled among oak trees with a surrounding forest.

"One of the pictures shows a portion of the dining room with fourteen tables. The dining room seated up to 150 people. The resort was open from May 1 to November 1, each year. Carriage service was provided to Willow Island to meet the train and bring people back and forth from the train. Rooms and meals cost from twelve to fourteen dollars a week.

"Advertisements for the resort boasted it as the best of food and service, plus an inexhaustible supply of healthful mineral water and an ideal place for comfort and rest."

Sonnencroft
by Don Reeves

The Sonnencroft Castle was built and occupied by the Clyde Effington Hutchinson family in Fairmont, West Virginia. The mansion stood at the corner of Morgantown Avenue and Mason Street.

The castle was copied after the Scottish castle, Inverness. Mrs. Hutchinson saw this castle on a trip to Scotland and, on returning, employed the architects, Holboe and Lafferty of Clarksburg, West Virgin-

Sonnencroft Castle

ia, to model a structure similar to Inverness for the Hutchinson family in 1910.

Sonnencroft's "coming out" party was on New Year's Eve, 1914. It is reported that four hundred persons attended.

The floor plans shown in this article were drawn by John W. (Jack) Hutchinson, grandson of Clyde Hutchinson. Also included are his recollections of the mansion and the grounds that surrounded this lavish home.

SURROUNDINGS

The Sonnencroft Castle sat on eleven acres of land with the frontage on Morgantown Avenue. Approximately five acres of land was landscaped and included formal gardens. The cut stone wall surrounding the property was built by Mrs. Hutchinson's father, Jacob M. Watkins, a widely known stonemason in the area.

The name Sonnencroft, which means "home of sons" in German, was given to the home by Miss Susan Moore, a friend of the family. The

Sonnencroft at its finest.

home was also known as the haunted house, the Hutchinson Mansion, and the Hutchinson Castle.

Sonnencroft was built in 1912-1913. The basic construction was of hollow terra cotta tile faced with cement stucco. It had one square tower on the Mason Street end and one round tower on the front facing Morgantown Avenue on the west end. A second round tower was on the middle back wall.

The roof was flat with a built-up roofing covered with limestone chips.

Two driveways entered the property off Mason Street. These were also covered with limestone chips. The main driveway entrance to the mansion was lined with curved stucco walls, and the drive passed under the portico at the main porch where high concrete steps were constructed for dismounting from a horse or carriage. The driveway passed under the portico at the east end of the house and down a concrete graded slope through a tunnel winding to the lower end of the property on Morgantown Avenue near the Judge Harry Shaw Estate. The second driveway entered also off Mason Street and was the main access to a three car garage that had its own gasoline storage tank and hand pump. The garage also had a second floor apartment with four rooms and bath, and a basement with a fruit cellar where the apple crop was carefully wrapped in newspaper and stored on open slatted racks to keep indefinitely.

There was a large sliding barn door in the back of the garage opening to a garden equipment storage area. Here a workbench held tools necessary for upkeep of equipment needed to operate the estate.

Connecting the garage to the main house was a grape arbor with a prolific grape vine entwined over its top and sides. This arbor covered a six foot wide concrete walkway centered by a "pergola" or gazebo as they were sometimes called. The pergola had latticed walls covered with fragrant flowering vines of wisteria, morning glory and colorful clematis. The floor of the pergola was fifteen feet square and paved with quarry tile. There were wooden benches where the ladies of the house spent many leisure hours "taking the air."

A sickle pear tree, said to be over a hundred years old in 1930, grew at one side of the walk from the pergola to the kitchen porch. Other trees on the property were two Ginkgo trees near the dining room, catalpa, maples, oaks, sycamore, and two rows of magnificent magnolia trees. These bordered the formal gardens on the west side of the house. There were also golden and red delicious apple trees, peach, cherry, and damson plums.

The property was bordered by a solid mass of flowering shrubs abundant with blossoms each spring. All the buildings were nearly half-covered with English ivy.

North of the garage was a barn of stucco with a flat roof. Inside was the area for wagon and carriage, two stalls for cows and an area for the storage of food for the livestock. Its second floor contained a small apartment.

Behind the barn, a two level chicken house contained 1,000 chickens during the depression years. The garden in back produced fresh vegetables during the summer and provided canning by servants, and later, by the ladies of the house.

The formal Italian gardens bloomed in the area in the west of the mansion with an entrance from the conservatory. The first level was about ten feet below the house level. The garden area of approximately seventy by fifty feet was arranged in about fourteen flower beds placed symmetrically around a circular disk of grass centered with a sundial. There were four foot wide limestone chip walkways with one foot wide strips of grass bordering the flower beds. The second level was mostly a grassed area with flower bed borders. A rock garden boasted a large boulder transported from Smithtown, Mr. Hutchinson's boyhood home, over which water poured to a stone-lined waterway and into a fifteen foot kidney-shaped lily pond shaded by a giant weeping willow tree.

FIRST FLOOR

The house measured approximately one hundred feet long. Its west end was about sixty-five feet while the northeast wing was about fifty feet long and eighteen feet wide.

There were two porches on the east end of the house, plus a kitchen porch. The main open porch was reached from the first driveway and held a wicker swing and chairs and tables to provide comfort on a hot summer day. A fiber rug covered the floor.

A thirty foot long sun porch which opened to the billiard room and library also contained wicker furniture. This was the most used entrance to the home.

The front entrance to Sonnencroft, although little used by the family, was on the Morgantown Avenue side. One entered the property by means of a six foot wide curved stairway which leveled and turned to-

Southeast Corner

wards the house with six steps more taking it to the walkway. Electric lanterns at this entrance illuminated dark nights.

At the front entrance six steps led to the landing. The landing was flanked on either side by curved concrete benches. Huge urns filled with plantings rested on top of the walls bordering the entrance. Large white double doors led into the house from the porch. An overhanging balcony, off a second floor bedroom, protected the porch and provided a pleasing spot to inspect the grounds.

Over the top of the doors was a leaded glas window which provided light for the hall inside. The main hall, seventeen by twenty-four feet, (where dances were held) had a coat closet on both sides.

A heavy chandelier of bronze hung from the center of the main hall. At the left stood a large chest flanked by two blue velvet chairs, with low backs and heavy arms. Over the chest was an antique portrait of a Stuart-type George Washington. To the right of the entrance was a graceful, yet sturdy, oak console with a mirror over it. The hallway along with the entire house had hardwood floors. These were covered by the most part with oriental rugs.

Opposite the entrance was a four foot wide open stairway which ascended to the second floor. A second four foot stairway descended to the lower level. The landing halfway up the upper stairway was about eighteen feet long and five feet wide. The landing wall facing the hall was paneled in dark oak. Opposite this was a balustrade over which one could look down to the basement or up to the second floor ceiling. At the right of the landing was a twenty-two foot high stained glass window bearing the Scottish motto "East, West — Home's Best."

Returning to the main entrance hall, the first door on the right led to a thirteen by thirteen foot library. Here, walls were lined with shelved bookcases with leaded glass doors at the bottom and open tops on which three Aladdin lamps with candle flame bulbs sat. A long heavy table was here, as was a gray knobby-looking tapestry love seat. A matching chair was in the corner.

Passing the library, one entered the billiard room complete with a full sized billiard table. The walls were of sand-finished plaster with a dish rail around the upper third of the wall. The end wall contained a dark red, brick-faced fireplace.

Over the mantle was a bas-relief, cast in plaster, of Paul Revere and his dog. On either side of the fireplace hung plaster bulldog heads. In the front corner of this room, which was the ground floor of the square tower, was an antique pump organ. The heavy oak furniture in this room was leather covered. A 1921 model radio with huge knobs and a horn speaker sat on an oak game table. Both the billiard room and the library had French door entrances from the sun porch.

At the left of the main hall entrance was a door to a thirty-five foot long by eighteen foot wide living room. Its southwest corner was the base of the round tower which was sixteen feet in diameter. The three doors leading to the living room were of double sliding pocket style. One door opened to the hall, one to the conservatory and one to the music room. The west wall of the living room held a large wood-burning fireplaced faced with copper colored tiles in the design of fleur-de-lis and Scottish shields. In the tower area stood a large oak drop-front desk. Over this desk hung a portrait of Mr. Hutchinson painted by a Russian painter, a Mr. Neisbert. Mrs. Hutchinson's picture hung opposite that of her husband. Lighting in the living room was from lamps and wall sconces. No center light was in the living room.

The music room, which could be entered from the living room, was about sixteen by sixteen feet. The west wall of the music room was of glass, and French doors opened into the conservatory.

The dining room was twenty-five feet long and twenty-three feet wide. Its north wall held a white tiled fireplace with a white hearth. Mirrored panels hung over the mantle and on either side were cupboards with leaded glass doors at the top. The cupboards held mirrors in the back for reflections. Paneled doors at the cupboard bases concealed storage for silver and linens. At the east end of the room was a long buffet. A long table that seated about thirty persons centered the room.

The conservatory, entered from outside, was sixteen feet square. In the center of the room was a round six foot diameter pool. A statue of a small boy holding a duck stood in the pool. The duck spouted water into a bowl that spilled out into the pool. Many plants were around the conservatory. From the conservatory, French doors led into the formal gardens.

The northwest corner of the dining room was the back tower room. This was the breakfast room and contained furniture of mahogany. All the radiators in the house were covered with benches. Most of the windows had radiators underneath them.

House cleaning was simplified by a central vacuum system located in the basement with pipes running to each room with nozzles to which a vacuum hose could be attached.

From the breakfast room, swinging doors opened into the pantry with traditional wood cupboards and glass doors. The pantry doors opened into a twenty by fifteen foot kitchen where a huge old-fashioned gas stove dominated the room. The stove had three ovens plus a warming shelf at the top. Through the kitchen hall was the back porch, a maid's room, and the back stairs to the second floor and down to the laundry in the basement.

In the basement was also a twenty by thirty-six foot room that housed a fifteen by thirty foot swimming pool, shower and dressing room. To the left was a fruit cellar. Across the tunnel from the exit was the laundry room. There was also a boiler room with a large coal bin. The mansion burned seven tons per month during the winter.

SECOND FLOOR

On the second floor were nine bedrooms, plus a sleeping porch which accommodated ten or twelve in dormitory style. There was also a tower room with a bath on the third floor for servants. Also on this floor in the southeast corner wing with the square tower were what were known as the boy's bedrooms.

The southeast wing, second floor, had three bedrooms and a sleeping porch. The third floor tower room was used for trunk and luggage storage.

One bedroom in the center front was a guest room. The southwest

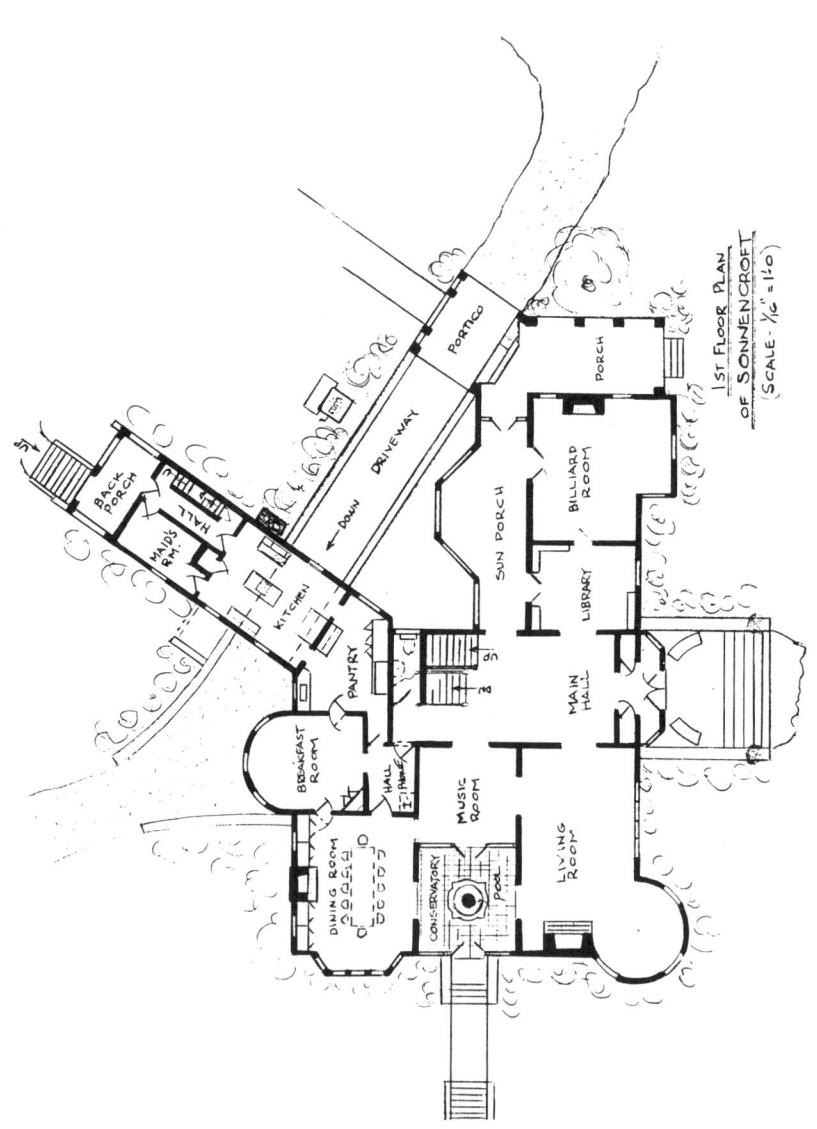

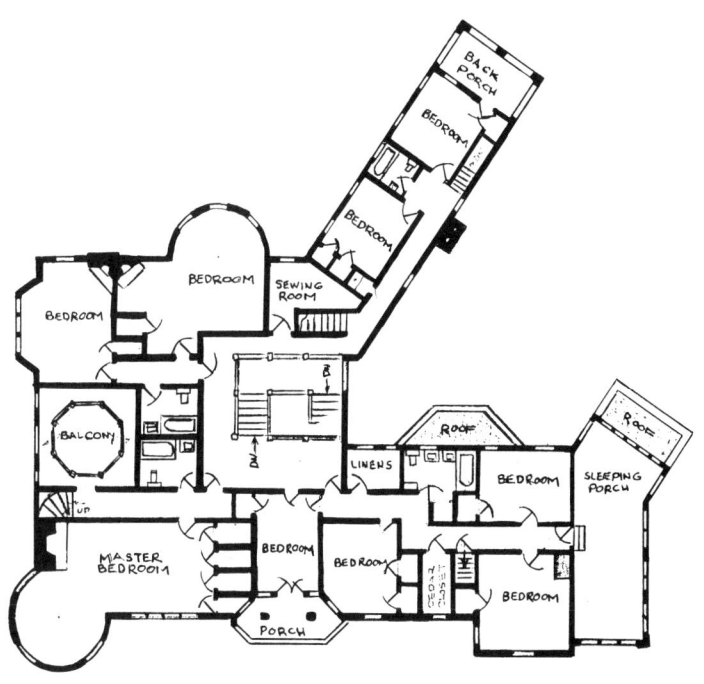

2ND FLOOR PLAN OF SONNENCROFT
(SCALE 1/16" = 1'-0")

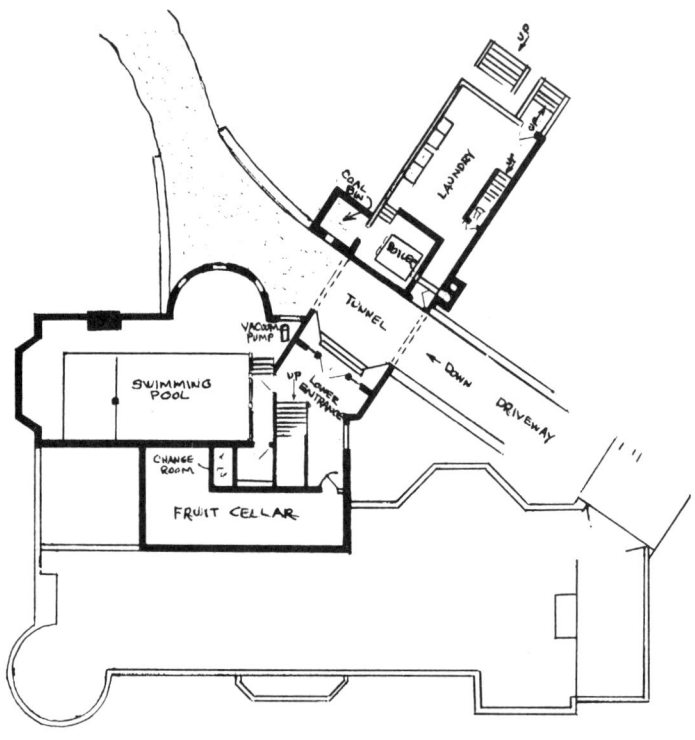

corner bedroom, which included the tower, was the master bedroom. It was fourteen by twenty-eight feet plus the tower area. It had a gas fireplace and four walk-in closets with mirrored doors. Three large tower windows and a continuous row of four windows were on the south wall of the master bedroom. In the same wing a curved stairway provided access to the third floor playroom.

Off the hallway was an entrance to the balcony over the conservatory. Most bedrooms had baths attached. The northwest wing had two guest rooms with one bath including the tower. They were sixteen by twenty feet and nineteen by fifteen feet. Each had a corner gas fireplace. Opposite the railing over the main hallway was a sewing room.

Sonnencroft being dismantled by firemen on May 25, 1960.

Mrs. Thelma Shaw

by Kelley Baxter and Kelley Creel

Sonnencroft was an elaborate home built in Fairmont, West Virginia during the coal boom of the early nineteen hundreds. It was fashioned after a Scottish castle, and built by the Hutchinson family of Fairmont. During the stock market crash, the Hutchinson family had to sell their "castle" for financial reasons. Judge Harry Shaw along with Colonel Sperry of Clarksburg, West Virginia, purchased the home. Following Judge Shaw's death, Mrs. Thelma Shaw inherited the home and was left with the burden of a rapidly declining property. Mrs. Shaw agreed to share with us her memories of the mansion's glory and its demise.

"Sonnencroft was the name given to the house that was built on the hill next to us by Mr. and Mrs. C.E. Hutchinson which is supposed to mean 'house of many sons.' It was fashioned after the Scottish castle, Inverness. Sonnencroft is known more familiarly now as the Hutchinson mansion. It was built before I came to Fairmont and, I assume, had reached its peak during the great coal boom in Marion County. In fact, Mr. Hutchinson, who lived in it, was one of the leading producers of coal here. The idea of the name for the house probably originated with Mrs. Hutchinson who was the former Lydia Watkins and the mother of eight sons.

"She and Mrs. Hutchinson visited Scotland in 1910, and in 1912 they began the task of constructing Sonnencroft. I am told that a fashionable ball on New Year's Eve marks the opening of Sonnencroft. It

Mrs. Thelma Shaw

was a romantic castle with many large rooms, closets and cubicles—truly an imposing place.

"A conservatory ran the entire height of the house. There was a paneled balcony encircled by a railing on the second floor. I remember the elaborately carved woodwork that was around that balcony. The house had twenty-five large rooms and every modern convenience of the day one could imagine. There were outside buildings, including a garage whose second floor provided extra housing for the help.

"There was a swimming pool in the basement then, a very unusual feature for houses in this area. Strangely enough, later on when my family was part owner, the fact that there was little basement space, other than the pool, made it difficult to plan for extensive repairs.

"The grounds around the house were terraced and planted with beautiful magnolia trees, white birches and variety of fine shrubbery."

"The Hutchinsons were victims of the financial crash of 1929. Some time thereafter the house was sold at the Marion County Courthouse for back taxes.

"Judge Shaw learned that the owner of an outdoor theatre and other commercial entrepreneurs were interested in buying the property. To protect his own adjoining property, he looked into the idea of acquiring it. Before making definite plans, Judge Shaw asked Mr. Brooks Hutchinson, the eldest son and an attorney, if any of the family intended bidding it in. If so, he would have relinquished doing so himself. None of the Hutchinsons evidenced any intention of bidding, thus leaving Judge Shaw and Colonel Sperry of Clarksburg free to make the purchase.

"Sonnencroft was not even then in completely good rapair. The Hutchinson family continued to live there quite some time after the sale. Finally, the new owners, unable to rent so large and expensive-to-maintain property to a single responsible individual, decided to convert it into apartments. Subsequently, three different architects were employed to determine if such conversion would be possible, practicable, or financially feasible. One by one, the three architects' reports were negative.

"Though the spectacular design of the ivy-covered house was that of an impressive castle, the structure itself was not built in such a way as to accommodate the anticipated necessary repairs without enormous expense and considerable rebuilding. The hoped-for conversion was not possible.

"Tenants in the outside buildings were charged with guarding the empty property. But thieves, vandals, vagrants, and even supposedly reputable townspeople, began destructive raids until it became unsightly and a virtual shell that was a target for the invasion of students at a nearby high school during their noon hour, at considerable risk of life and limb.

"I used to worry myself sick over these things, and I am sure that some of my gray hairs came about because of constant fears of serious injury to someone, as well as the frustration of my futile efforts to stop the vandalism and vagrants.

"Before Judge Shaw's death in the early 50's, he had been asked by the board of education to sell Sonnencroft for an extension of their adjacent land. He agreed to consider sale at a low price because of his long association in years past with the school.

"He died before the transaction was consummated. As beneficiary of my father-in-law's will, I became the owner of Sonnencroft. Eventually, I sold it to the board of education with the stipulation that the house be razed as soon as possible.

"It had become a community eyesore, a place of danger, an ever-increasing source of personal worry, and above all, an 'unattractive nuisance' that made me quite vulnerable to legal action. So, what was left of Sonnencroft was razed.

"In this connection, I never publicly explained the situation and events that led to this decision. It was perhaps natural that rumors sprang up about the property. There was gossip that my family and the previous owners were enemies, so that morbid satisfaction was felt in seeing the house fall down about its own ears. This was patently ridiculous! More recently, the newspaper *Hillbilly* gave a romanticized account of Sonnencroft and deplored the action of those responsible for its demise.

"I am that person. But I had no other choice, really! Neither I nor anyone else could have restored Sonnencroft at that moment in time.

"I only know that I was painfully aware of my responsibility for maintaining what had, indeed, become an 'attractive nuisance.' I felt a sadness, but a certain relief, when it was removed before anyone was seriously hurt."

Sonnencroft in its final days, after vandals and vagrants had taken their toll.

Mrs. Hutchinson sold the property and moved to a house on Gaston Avenue in October of 1934. The Marion County Board of Education was the final owner of the property, and the house was dismantled on May 25, 1960 by the Fairmont city firemen.

APPENDIX
Index of Students

Janet Affolter
Fred Anderson
Deneene Arthurhults
Kenny Armstrong
Ann Bailey
Matilda Bailey
Mary barlow
Betsy Barger
Kelly Baxter
Linda Bays
Brian Bee
Steve Bell
Mike Bostaph
Andy Brooks
John Bryant
Margaret Butler
Lisa Carpenter
Joan Carte
Robert Chichester
Brian Clegg
George Coury
Mary Cox
Carla Criss
Cheri Criss
Rebecca Criss
Billy Crites
Kelly Creel
Katherine Curkendall
Brian Davis
Claudia Denton
Emily Dukas
Nancy Dykhoff
Karen Easton
Alora Edgell
Mike Edwards
Eli Ellison
Randy Evans
Terrye Evans
Terri Farell
Linda Farrah
Lisa Farrah
Eric Fletcher
JoAnn Fletcher
Russ Fornash
Rex Foster
Brett Francisco
Brenda Goddard
Robert Griffith
Kellie Grimm
Lori Hall
Brian Halley
Lori Harpold
Brenda Henline
Kamilyn Irvin
Leslie Johnson
Jennifer Johnston
Jenny Jones
Julie Kelley
Terri Kress
Karen Kuhl
David Kurtz
Pamela Lane
Bill Leech
Drema Lemley
Ed Leon
Peggy Lieving
Jeff Life
Steve Lockhart
James Longwell
Tina Lowers
Mick McFarland
Robert McNemar
Barri Marshall
Donna Martin
Lisa Martin
Mike Mason

Fred Mayer
Joseph Mays
Martin Meador
Linda Miller
Margarite Miller
Judy Moat
Donna Mollahan
Scott Morgan
Scott Morehead
Mark Nesselroad
Debbie Nutter
Steve Parks
Tim Parks
Sherri Parsons
Terry Peck
Laura Plummer
Mike Postlewaite
Karen Powell
Robin Rader
Mike Ransbottom
Don Reeves
Kelly Riel
Jeff Roberts
Tim Roberts
Mary Rollefson
Eric Ruf
Chris Rust
Roberta Russell
Mike Samuels

Mary Sargent
Janet Sayre
John Schneid
Carolyn Schwab
Teresa Scott
Amanda Seaman
Scott Seaman
Jane Shepherd
Mark Shinn
Dan Sirko
Jennifer Simon
Carla Simons
Bill Snyder
Susan Southall
Paula Starkey
Alan Stephens
Ryan Swisher
Cindy Terry
Craig Tanner
Richard Thirouin
Samual Thirouin
Mark Travis
Joe Trembly
Steve Wade
Leslie Waltzer
Gail Williamson
Judy Wilson
Barbara Whipkey
Steve Whittington

Index of Contacts

Ada Allen
Pauline Ash
W. M. Ball
Anna Ballie
Freda Ballie
Gertrude Ballie
O. C. Beckner

Paul Blazavich
Robert Blevins
Emily Blythe
Earl Booth
Anna Brochick
Alda Buczek
Louise Butcher

Jennings Butler
Clare Carpenter
Walter Carpenter
Vic Childers
J. G. Coe
Robert Clark
Rose Cooper
Spencer Creel
Carl Criss
Haskell Cunningham
Marvin Curkendall
Bill Currey
Ansil Cutlip
Garnet Dailey
Tom Dailey
Virgil Danley
Nina Danko
Pauline Darrah
Bradford Davis
H. L. Deever
Vicki Dils
Burt Dixon
Ora Dowler
Virginia Duckworth
Eurward Duffield
Marvin Dunbrach
Helen Elston
Robert Exline
Thelma Exline
Russ Fagen
Francis Fleming
Ray Fought
Lovenia Frame
Patrick Gainer
Garnett Sheers
Ed Garvey
Gary George
Carl Givens
Markwood Gum
Charles Hanna

Bill Harper
Roscoe Haverty
Dewey Helmick
Ed Hiehle
Howard Holtzworth
Helen Huddleston
Jack Hutchinson
Francis Inslee
Willard Jackson
Ben Johnston
Geraldine Jones
Myrtle Jones
Nelly Kelly
Mason Kisamore
Susan Klimas
Walter Layman
Charles Leavitt
Ray Lemley
Harry Leeper
Helen Light
Lester Lind
Chester Lyon
Mary McBride
Bessie McCauley
Larry McCoy
Dianna McMahan
Scott McMillen
Bill McNeel
Margaret Meredith
Pearle Merryman
Alvin Moore
Virginia Moser
Mr. & Mrs. Moyers
Roy Murphy
Richard Neale
Oral Nicholson
Harold Nestler
Ralph Nutter
Virgie Otterbein
Clara Powell

Bill Reed
Jack Reese
Ethel Reynolds
Paul Rice
Gladys Richards
John Richards
Georgiana Robbins
Bill Roberts
Jerald Rogers
Nobel Schofield
Henderson Sharp
Thelma Shaw
James Shaver
Garnett Shears
Pearl Siron
Beauchamp Smith
Orpha Stalnaker
Joseph States
Carl Stephens

Virginia Sturm
Jack Terrell
Emmett Taylor
Martha Taylor
Lottie Thompson
James Thompson
Burton Thorne
Jack Tyrell
Earl Uhl
Pearl Ward
Frederick Way
Helen White
Bertha Wilson
Woodrow Wilson
Tommy Windsor
Joyce Wines
Edelene Wood
Lee Young

Glossary

The following glossary is an excerpt from *Tumult on the Mountains* by Roy B. Clarkson. This book gives a general overview of the early timber industry and a pictorial guide to the early logging operations.

A

ark - Name applied in West Virginia to the floating houses used for cooking, eating, or sleeping, in river driving. There was usually a single ark for the cookhouse and dining room, one for the bunkhouse, and one for the horses. The latter was called a horse-flat.

B

ball-hammer - A small hammer carried on the harness hames used for knocking out balls of ice and snow that formed under a horse's shoes.

ballhooter - One who rolls logs down a hillside.

barker - One who peels bark in gathering tanbark. Syn. peeler, spudder.

batteau - Small boat used on river drives.

bohunk - 1. A hammer carried on the harness hames by means of a loop. It was used by the teamster to cut the trail of logs when out of sight of the grab driver. 2. Name applied to Italians and Austrians.

break a landing - To roll a pile of logs from a landing into the water.

to brush a road - To cover with brush the mudholes and swampy places in a skid road, to make it solid.

buck - To cut a tree into logs of suitable length after it has been felled.

bunk - 1. A lumberjack's bed. 2. The crossbeam on a log car upon which stringers for the floor of the car rests.

C

cant hook - A tool similar to a peavey but having a toe-ring and lip at the end instead of a pike. Used to roll and lift logs. This term was often used in West Virginia to denote a peavey.

carriage - Part of a sawmill that holds the logs and carries them past the saw.

cookee - Assistant cook and dishwasher in a logging camp.

cook shack - Kitchen.

corks - Short, sharp metal spikes placed in the soles of loggers' boots to prevent slipping when walking on logs, ice, etc. Syn. calks, caulks.

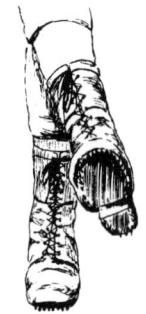

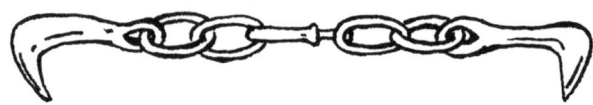

coupler - A device consisting of two iron hooks fastened together by four links with a swivel in the middle. Used to fasten logs together in a trail. Syn. grab.

crosscut saw - A two-man saw used to fell and buck trees. Syn. briar.

crotch grabs - Two grabs hooked by short chains to one ring thus forming a V.

D

deck - 1. A pile of logs in the woods at a landing. 2. Platform in a sawmill where logs roll to await sawing.

dog - 1. A short, heavy piece of steel, bent and pointed at one end and with an eye or ring at the other. 2. A hook on the carriage of a band sawmill used to hold logs. 3. Various pointed pieces of metal attached to rings or chains and used in constructing log rafts and booms.

dogger - Man who rides the carriage in a band sawmill and sets the dogs in place to hold a log while it is being sawed.

double-bitted ax - An ax with a sharp blade on two sides.

drive - 1. To float logs from the forest to the mill. 2. Body of logs in the process of being floated from the forest to the mill.

E

edger - Machine in a sawmill designed to trim the edges of a board to make them square and of standard width.

edgings - Scraps cut off a board by the edger.

F

filer - 1. One who files the crosscut saws in the woods. 2. One who files saws in a band mill. Syn. saw filer.

fitter - One who notches the tree for felling, and after it is felled marks the log lengths into which it is to be cut.

G

gee - Command given to horses or oxen directing them to move to the right.

grab maul - A hammer often made by the blacksmith and used to pound grabs or couplers into logs.

grab skipper - Hammer with a pointed end or ends used to knock out grabs or couplers from logs.

H

haul - The distance and route over which teams must go between two given points, as between the woods and the landing.

haw - Command given to a team to indicate a turn to the left.

hick - Lumberjack. Woodhick.

to horse logs - In river driving, to drag stranded logs back to the stream by the use of peaveys.

J

java - Coffee.

jerk water - Coffee.

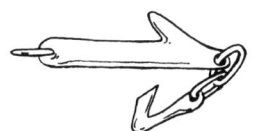 

J-grab - Special type of grab or coupler used on steep slopes. This type of grab permits the skidding team to step aside (jay-off), become disengaged and stand while the logs continue down the slope. Syn. J-hook.

jay-hole - Space prepared along a skidway to permit a team to jay-off while logs run by.

jay-off - When a team steps aside to allow running logs to pass by.

K

key log - In river driving, a log which was so wedged that it caused a jam to form.

knot bumper - Man who cuts limbs from a felled tree. This work is done with a double-bitted or a poleax.

L

landing - A place to which logs are hauled or skidded and piled to await transportation by rail or water to the sawmill.

lobby - Room in a logging camp where the men congregated after meals, before bedtime, on Sundays, etc.

lobby hog - Man who carried coal, swept floors, built fires, lit lamps, and did a multitude of other chores. Usually an undesirable job.

log berries - Prunes.

log-scaler - Man who measures the board feet contained in a log by using a log rule.

log slide - A V-shaped trough built down a slope for the purpose of sliding logs to a landing at the bottom.

N

nigger - A rapidly moving device on the carriage in a sawmill that turns the logs for sawing. It was usually operated by steam.

notch - 1. To make an undercut in a tree preparatory to felling it. 2. The undercut made in a tree to direct its direction of fall.

P

peavey - A stout wooden lever, from 5 to 7 feet long, fitted at the larger end with a metal socket, a pike, and a curved steel hook which works on a bolt; used in handling logs, in river driving and in rolling logs on a landing.

punk - 1. Light bread. 2. Young man. 3. Rotten wood.

punkies - Gnats.

R

ritchie - Heavy woolen clothes worn by the lumberman.

river boss - The foreman in charge of a log drive.

river driver - One who works on a log drive.

river hog - A name for river drivers.

S

scaler - One who measures the volume of logs.

setter - Man who rides on the carriage and controls the setworks.

shay - A geared locomotive manufactured by Lima Locomotive Works or its successors of Lima, Ohio. Syn. stemwinder.

skid-road - A road or trail used to drag logs over from stump to landing.

slash, n. - The limbs and tops left after logging. Syn. slashing.

splash dam - A dam built to store a head of water for driving logs. Usually used in a small stream.

spud - A tool for removing bark. Used especially in barking hemlock for tanbark.

spudder - One who removes hemlock bark from logs.

swamp - To clear the ground of underbrush, fallen trees and other obstructions in preparation for construction of a skid-road.

swamper - One who swamps.

switchback - Railroad constructed in such a way as to allow the train to be pulled up a mountain hollow then by proper switching the engine pushed from behind while climbing the steepest grades. This allowed log trains to go up extremely steep mountains.

T

teamster - A man who drives a team of horses in skidding logs.

turkey - A bag containing a lumberjack's personal belongings.

two streaks of rust - A logging railroad.

W

wedge a tree - To cause a tree that is partially sawed to fall by using wedges.

widow-maker - A broken limb hanging loose in the top of a tree.

Y

yeast under him - Expression used when a man was fired.